UNCLE JIM'S JUNGLE STORIES

The Jungle Adventures of a Missionary Kid

James R. Cook

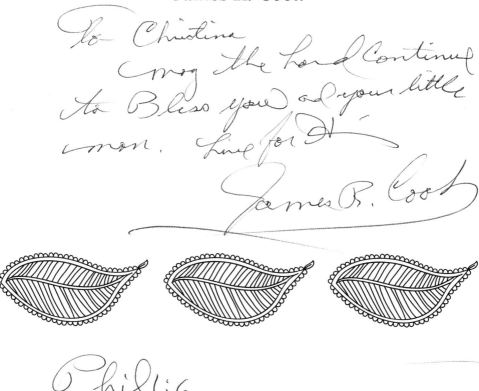

To Christina
may the Lord continue
to Bless you and your little
man. Live for H—

James R. Cook

Phil 1:6

All illustrations by Michal Strawbridge.

ISBN: 978-1-929862-86-3

Dedication

I would like to dedicate this book to the memory of my parents, John William and Jennie Cook, for their tremendous contribution to the Kingdom of God in a far-flung corner of the world.

I would also like to express my great appreciation and love to my wife, Shirley. Without her help this would not have been accomplished. My great thanks to our sons and their wives, Jim and Barb, John and Dee, for their encouragement to write these stories and place them in a book so they could be remembered for the future. Our grandchildren have listened to these stories many times through the years and, I'm sure will read them to their children.

My great appreciation goes to the Lord for His protection and deliverance so many times in my life. My mother said that the Lord had assigned me at least two guardian angels or I certainly would not have survived!

What a privilege it has been to be a missionary kid growing up in the jungles of India and then having had the opportunity of serving the Lord in ministry for an incredible 60 years.

Acknowledgement

Michal Strawbridge, a new and creative type of artist, has interpreted these Jungle Stories with tremendous authenticity. She does artistic work for Hume Lake Christian Camps. She, along with her husband, Kit, minister at Hume Lake where he directs the Junior program in which all the campers live in covered wagons for their week of camp. It is a tremendous ministry to young people.

I am thrilled to have had this artist contribute her talented artwork so that all may enjoy envisioning every story realistically as they are read.

About the Author

Dr. James R. Cook was born on September 2, 1930 in the little town of Truman, Minnesota. When he was about a year old he went with his parents to India where he lived until he was 13 years of age. His parents were pioneer missionaries in a remote part of North East India. Life was filled with many jungle adventures that imbedded themselves into his mind and life.

During the beginning years of World War II when the British government ordered all expatriate women and children to leave India he became a teenage refugee, along with his mother and two sisters. The adventure of leaving included weeks to cross India, being evacuated on a U.S. Navy ship, and finally ending up in a little place in Minnesota called Lake Crystal.

Young Jim finished high school in Lake Crystal. He excelled in athletics in high school, college and beyond, graduating from Northwestern College, at that time in Minneapolis, and Western Seminary in Portland, Oregon. Dr. Cook's ministry has been rich and full, first in youth ministry, then as a missionary, an international basketball coach, pastor, college and graduate school president and author, covering 60 years, with a special focus on young people and children.

He is blessed by his wife, Shirley, their two sons and wives, Jim and Barb and John and Dee, and their beautiful families, eight grandchildren and two great grandchildren.

For the last 15 years their ministry in preaching and teaching has led to various places in the U.S. and also internationally. His favorite Scriptures are Philippians 1:6 and 1:20.

In Praise of UNCLE JIM'S JUNGLE STORIES

"This new book by my friend Jim Cook captivated me. I literally couldn't put it down. He is a master story teller and has incredible stories to tell of life in India, as a child of pioneer missionaries. As I read I could not help but think how great it would have been to read these exciting stories of God's preservation of Jim's life to my children as they were growing up. His application of Biblical principles to those 'hair raising' events of life are deeply effective. And the best part—they are true! These events really happened to young Jim as the son of very effective missionaries that reach now into his own son, a third generation missionary. Unforgettable stories—every family will be enriched by reading this book."

TIM LAHAYE
Pastor
Author
National Christian Leader

"There is something very special about the word adventure. It creates thoughts of distant lands, hidden treasure, and the courage to travel into the unknown.

To read about adventure, stirs the blood and excites the mind. To view adventure through movies or television helps to expand the imagination.

Still even more exciting are the adventure stories that are true and have been lived out in real life. Jim Cook, descendent of the famous explorer Captain Cook, is one of those rare individuals who has personally experienced thrilling adventure from his childhood in India.

Jim has the unique ability to take true life adventures and make spiritual applications that apply to our daily life. Parents and children alike will be captivated by Uncle Jim's Jungle Stories."

BOB PHILLIPS, PHD
Executive Director for Hume Lake Christian Camps
New York Times Best Selling Author
Co-Founder of the Pointman Leadership Institute

"Oh, what wonderful stories Jim Cook has lived and written! These jungle tales should be read and re-read by parents, Sunday school teachers, home schoolers, and Christian school teachers—as well as any child or adult who enjoys well written, exciting and touching stories with a solid biblical message and practical, thoughtful life challenges. Somehow, on the page these true adventures are just as great as when Pastor Jim tells the tales! I couldn't recommend this delightful book more heartily."

DEE CAWOOD
Children's Librarian
Children's Ministry Leader
Grandma

"I enjoyed very much reading the stories my grandpa wrote. I remember hearing many of them as a child, and now reading them as an adult gave me a new understanding of this part of his life. They tell of the rustic encounters of a missionary life and document dramatic parallels between the rawness of the jungle and the deep reliance on faith to flourish in such an environment. When my children are older, I hope they, too, will enjoy reading these stories and recognize the enduring commitment of our missionary heritage."

CHRISTA HAFEMANN
Mother of 2
Granddaughter of Author

"This project has been an absolute joy. It was challenging, yet very rewarding. I am so grateful for the opportunity to be a part of bringing the truth of God's Word, and the sweetness of answering His call, to eager youngsters."

MICHAL STRAWBRIDGE
Artistic Interpreter for this book
Youth worker, speaker, art teacher,
Hume Lake Christian Camps

Contents

THE WORLD

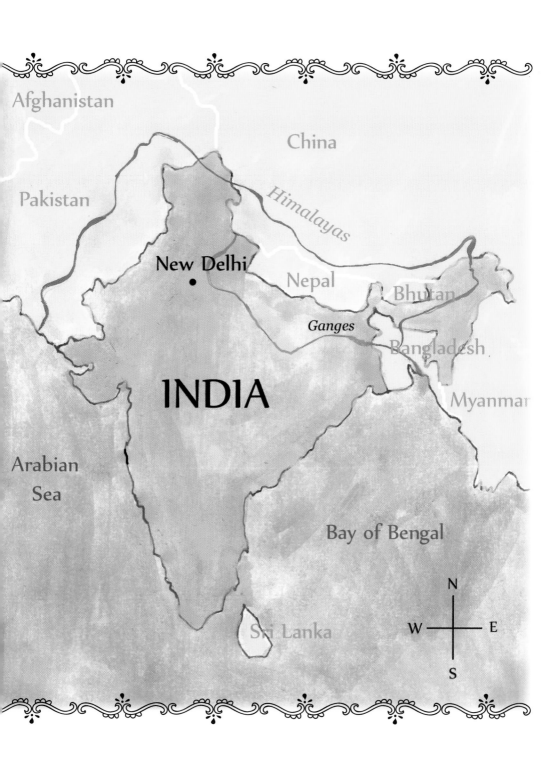

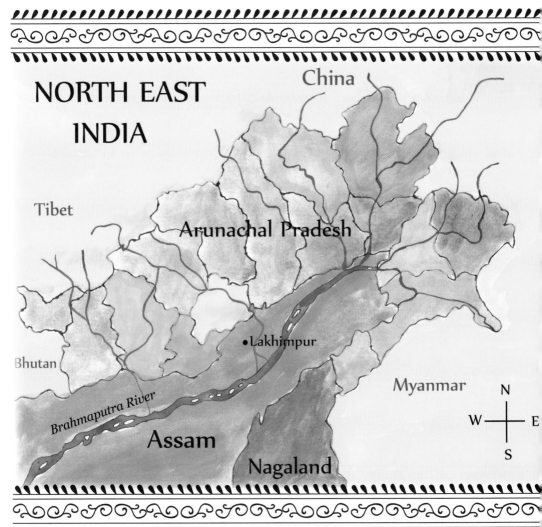

Introduction

In looking at our society the last number of years I have been increasingly surprised at what it takes to entertain people young and old. There is so little family time spent just being together eating, playing together and a time when each one in the family has a chance to tell a story or relate an experience. So often the privilege of listening to Grandpa or Grandma tell of their experiences and lessons they have learned from life is lost in the rapid pace of today's world. Today's young people want to hear from Grandpa and Grandma, so I felt it might be of help to have a book of stories from my life that are really quite different—stories that might put some adventure into the minds of young and old alike. I trust this book will entertain and be a blessing.

For many years I have been asked by my wife, my children and many others to write down some of the special stories from my childhood, early youth and later years. These stories are based on my experience and that of some of my friends. Others are based on things that happened to my parents and some of their missionary colleagues in India.

I will try to relate these true stories to the best of my remembrance, but I want you to realize that they took place when I was a young boy and include experiences from my lifetime of more than 70 years. For years I have told these stories to many individuals, many times in many places of the world. It is amazing that often when asked to come to give a series of messages in a church, the pastor will say to me that there is one requirement: I would need to give a jungle story every night for the kids before giving a message! Then he would say that he listened to the stories when he was a boy and they affected his life, and some of the lessons from these stories helped him with living his life and even have helped him as he went into the ministry. As I endeavor to put some of these stories down in book form, my prayer is that there will be something that will help each one. I trust that children and young people come to realize that they can depend on the Lord Jesus to care for them as they live. After having given their life to the Lord Jesus to control and direct, there can be assurance for and in their daily living. Even though these stories are very different than most young people live, yet the lessons of assurance and dependence can be applied to every life no matter where it is lived.

Most of these stories took place in Colonial India where I spent the first 13 years of my life. Others have taken place in my adult years as I have ministered in India and Sri Lanka. This gives you the backdrop for the area of the world where these experiences took place. As we embark together into these experiences I want you to think of *being there* and allow your imagination to take over and make you a part of the story. I trust you will be able to apply some of these jungle lessons to help you in your life's journey.

CHAPTER I

Journey Into the Unknown

My father and mother had volunteered to become missionaries and had spent many years getting ready for this calling. They both went to Northwestern College in Minneapolis, Minnesota, and my father also graduated from the University of Minnesota before doing his seminary work. They had wanted to go to Africa, but there was no opening for them at the time. My father became pastor of two little churches is southern Minnesota, First Baptist in Truman and Nashville Baptist, till an opening came available in Africa. It was amazing when an opening came, it was for India. They finally said to the Lord that they were willing to go even to India. I was born during their time in Minnesota, and the experience of my life began with our preparation to leave. There were many things that they had to do to get ready to go so far away.

I am often amazed at their commitment to go to India. Leaving their families was tremendously hard, I am sure. Both of them were totally ignorant of what was ahead of them, since neither one had ever been out of the country. Leaving security, friends and family was a test of their commitment to the Lord Jesus and the response to the great commission to "Go ye into all the world and preach the gospel" to all nations. So this is the beginning of a story of the lives of a little family being obedient to the Lord Jesus many years ago when the world was so very different than what it is today.

The trip to India was a tremendous experience for my folks who,

as I mentioned, had never been anywhere outside of the U.S.A. The trip across the country by train was amazing to these two farm people, and New York was astonishing. When they boarded the H.M.L. Laconia they were overwhelmed by the size of this great ship. Our family sailed from New York to Liverpool. The ocean was a tremendous experience for all of us. My mother enjoyed the trip the least of any of us because of being seasick. We finally arrived in Liverpool and my family was exposed to Great Britain and, for the first time, realized that they would be living under the monarchy that controlled the country of India, where they were going to serve.

After several days our family boarded the S.S. Mulbera for the long and arduous trip to India. Mother had one desire and that was to get the trip over with as quickly as possible. Finally we all arrived in the huge city of Madras in South India. I understand that the seas were very rough from Madras to Calcutta, but finally we all arrived. There we were met by one of the senior missionaries from a place called Sadiya, Assam, where my father and mother were to be assigned for their first year of language study. The trip from Calcutta to the northeast part of India took 18 hours by train and then by a river boat. We finally arrived at the mission outpost. As I said, I do not have any memory of this trip; I was just a year old. This place for language study was very far into North East India and *very* far from our American home.

My parents began studying the new language shortly after arriving in Sadiya. One day, as I was being looked after by a lady from the mission on the open back porch of our house, I became very excited when two black panthers came out of the jungle toward the porch and examined me closely. The lady who was taking care of me shrieked with fright and scared the two big, black cats back into the jungle. This was a frightening thing for my folks, especially when they learned that often these cats come to the edge of the village, snatch a child and run off into the jungle with the child who is never to be seen again. Needless to say, I was under much supervision after that incident!

There were many new and exciting things that our family experienced during this year. At its completion, my folks were assigned to a place called North Lakhimpur, which was about 150 miles up the Brahmaputra Valley. There were no railroads or direct roads to this location, only the different rivers to get there. Therefore we had to go by a number of different types

of boats. This took us into the deep jungle of that part of India. All of this was so very different for my folks because both of them came from farming country in the U.S.A. where this kind of jungle certainly did not exist. My father's father was a homesteader from Minnesota, and my mother came from a wealthy farmer's home in Iowa—and this was another planet to them, especially to my mother. They had answered the call to be missionaries in the frontier areas of North East India so this is how their missionary career started in 1931, and how it was that India became my home in the jungle.

As I said, I didn't know much about anything that took place, but looking back at this period as an adult I am amazed at the obedience of my parents, two servants of the Lord who were willing to go to the end—and I mean end—of the earth to bring the good news of salvation to those who had never heard. "Was it worth it?" you might ask, and I will have to say that the last chapter of this book will give you the accounting of this part of India becoming a very Christian part of the world, We would all have to say it was hard in many ways. As they faced separation, hardships, disease, danger and even death, it would seem *not* to be worth it, but the final results have attested to the fact that it *was*!

In the next chapter I will tell you a little bit about how we had to travel to get to our new jungle home.

ॐ

CHAPTER 2

River Journey to our Frontier Home

Upon completion of their year of language study my folks were looking forward to their placement in North Lakhimpur about 150 miles from Sadiya. To give you a picture of its location in India, it was about 800 miles northeast of Calcutta, in the very heart of the jungle! This remote place was the outpost of the missionary work in that part of India, and my parents were there alone. What a scary new adventure.

To get to North Lakhimpur from Sadiya, we first had to take a river boat, an English-built steamer, for a number of days up the Bramaputra River, which was luxury compared to the next boat. It must have been quite a sight to see what they were being transferred to. And *this* was called a *boat*? This boat was made up of two dugouts lashed together, with a bamboo platform built over the top of them. This platform was covered with a bamboo structure to house and protect us from the tropical sun and rain as we embarked on the rugged trip. My father had put all of our belongings on the boat and then put our mattresses on top of them. We would sleep at night, and my mother would sing to me and pray. It was very dangerous because when they would tie up to the bank, the jungle was just a few yards away. The boatman would be on the lookout for a tiger that might be coming to see what was of interest to him. The night times, I am told, were the most dangerous for that type of river travel. I am constantly amazed at my mother going into the unknown parts of a very strange country. By the way, may I mention again that I was just a year old at the time when all of this happened, so it's obvious that I got all of this information from my parents. In the years after I had returned as an adult I realized what a tremendous feat this was for our family. I have nothing but admiration for my parents.

This little boat became our home for several weeks as we journeyed into the far interior of this magical world. It was magical because the river was full of intrigue with great crocodiles in it, and on the shore were wild elephants and rhinos that could be seen as we traveled up the river. The reason why it took so long was because there was no motor, and the boat was polled up the river with long bamboo poles! It was a new experience living on a little boat with native boatmen speaking a language my parents had just begun to understand. They proceeded up the river to what they must have thought to be the end of the world! They were totally alone in a world they did not know, with people they had to trust would take them to the right destination. This was the beginning of an incredible new chapter in their lives. I can only imagine my parents living with these men on that crude little boat with all the normal activities of life going on, especially for my mother. Here she was with the husband she loved and her little son in a totally foreign world, realizing *now* more fully the cost of having said yes to the Lord and to my father. What a lady!

Finally we arrived at a little river village and went by several heavily loaded oxcarts through the jungles till we finally came to our new home in the village called North Lakhimpur. We moved into our home, which was built on stilts and had a thatch roof, and it took much work to make this place livable for us. The yard was cut right out of the jungle, and I am sure that made my mother very apprehensive. The jungle was 100 feet from the house. We had many animal visitors from this jungle in our yard at night. The different noises that we heard were especially intriguing after going to bed, but that is another story for other chapters.

There was much work to be done by my father and mother, to make this place a home for us. Among the first things that my father did was to screen in the verandah in the front of the house and every window to try to keep the mosquitoes out of our lives! This was very important because of the malaria they carried which killed many people in this jungle region. Then he attached canvas under the roof of thatch and secured it so those creatures that lived in the thatch would be separated from *us* living down below!

The third thing that my father did was to use jute and force it into the cracks between the boards of the floor. Then he took some tar and poured is over the jute, sealing the entire floor. After that they waxed the boards with some very special wax. I do not know what it was called but I know that the boards shined. Then my mother placed some striking tribal throw rugs around the entire floor. It looked very beautiful. By the way, these floors were sawed mahogany boards from trees that had been felled from the surrounding jungle. After all of this, my father and some workers created a yard for the family to have a play area. In the process of doing this the workers killed 17 cobras. This was another cause for anxiety for my mother!

This unique place was our home in the frontier area of the jungle where I was raised. Looking back, I have some very fond memories of things that took place there. Even though we lived in the jungle and had only kerosene lamps, every Friday night my mother would put on a white table cloth, get out her beautiful Czechoslovakian crystal and silver, and place candles on the table to have a candlelight dinner for her family. She said that even though we lived in the jungle we needed to learn proper American customs. So you see, even in the jungle I had proper bringing up.

This house became a home because of the care my parents put into making it a special place to house their family. My mother used to say to all the missionaries that a home had to be made so that all could function well and have a safe and secure place for the family to live.

Again I am taken by the depth of commitment that my parents made with their lives to serve the Lord Jesus. Their dedication in carrying the message of salvation to those who would never have had the opportunity to hear, had *they* not gone, is awe inspiring. This was the dedication that I witnessed as I grew up and, subsequently, the backdrop of my life that followed.

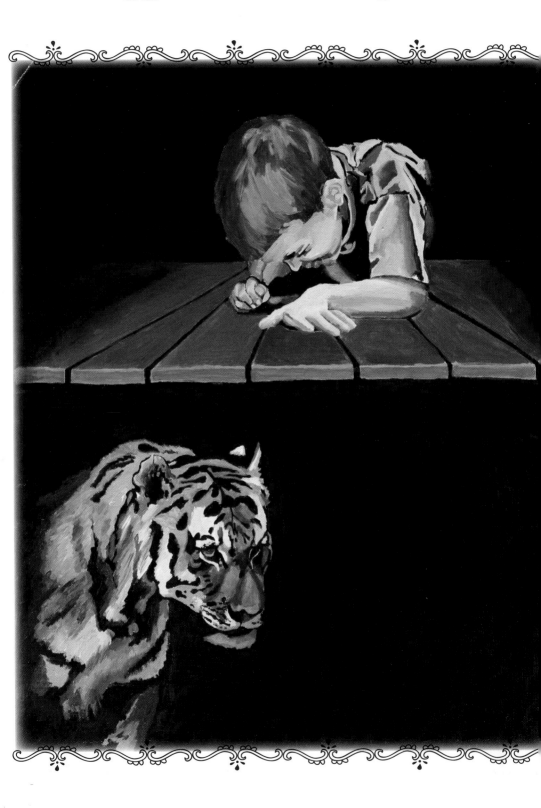

CHAPTER 3

Our Jungle Home and a Tiger's Visit

As I grew up in my jungle home, life was filled with excitement and adventure.

One of my first languages was Assamese; I spoke it, along with several other languages, a long time before I spoke English. I had many new friends in the village and I became a little Indian, I guess. Many things happened during those days, but one I remember was my first experience with a real Bengal tiger.

In my home I had a little bedroom on one side in the back of the house not far from my parents' room. At night we would have many visitors from the jungle. Even though there was a fence around our compound, that didn't stop the animals of the jungle from coming into our compound and then coming under our house!

When it was time to go to bed I often would hear the jackals start to howl under the house. Jackals are much like coyotes in our country that howl as they gather together. It was an awful racket, which made it hard to think of going to sleep, but that was the jungle serenade for all of us. One night the jackals were very restless under the house. All of a sudden they scattered in every direction. I climbed out of my bed and got down on my stomach on the floor, where I had made a little hole between the planks that made up our floor, and started looking to see what was coming. Suddenly the silence was broken with a low growl—and before I knew it I was looking at the form of a tremendous tiger! The moon was quite bright so that the form of that big tiger was very clear. My heart jumped into my throat and started to pound very fast. That big cat stopped and looked around in every direction. He then growled again and seemed to look up at me. My skin prickled and I felt frozen, hoping that he could not see me! I was thankful that my father had taken great precautions in protecting every opening into the house so that I felt quite secure to a point, until I was looking down at a royal Bengal tiger that was only five or six feet from me! This somehow left me feeling totally at his mercy. I was so scared I started to shake. I jumped into my bed and covered my head, and prayed that the big cat would go back into the jungle!

As I lay in my bed listening, I heard the breathing and some growls, and then slowly his growling got farther away as he left the area, going back into the jungle. I will tell you that for my first experience with the king of our jungle, I realized that this was *his* kingdom and *I* would have to be very careful if I were going to live to be an older person!

The next morning I asked my father and mother if they had heard anything in the night. They both looked at each other and said that they had heard the tiger under our house and were concerned but felt our jungle home was quite secure.

After breakfast my father and I went below the house and discovered the tracks of a very large tiger indeed. By this time many people from the village came to talk with my father about a big tiger that came through the village during the night. Fortunately nobody was killed that night. In the months that followed there were several people who were killed by a tiger that became known as a man eater and would have to be killed.

This was one of many experiences with tigers that I had while growing up in the jungles of North East India for the first years of my life. I have thought of that home and how it was a protection for my family in the midst of the jungle. It was not a strong house compared to the houses we live in today, but it was a place of protection and safety.

I am reminded that we often feel vulnerable as we face life. Think of all the areas of danger we face every day even in our country where all seems so safe. Then as we hear the news and all the problems around us, I want to remind each of us of one great truth. That truth is related to the fact that the Lord Jesus can and will be our protector if we will let Him. First of all we must come to grips with the need to make Him our Savior by accepting Him as our personal pardon for sin and then asking Him to be the Lord in and of our lives.

As we read the papers and watch television news we are often reminded that we live in a different kind of a jungle. Often I think that this jungle is much more dangerous than the one in which I grew up. We must always remember that the Scripture reminds us that He is our refuge and strength and a very present help when we are in trouble. Because of all this, keep your life close to the instructions the Lord has given us through His Word and walk in constant communication with Him. Pray and plan your life depending on the one that has said "I will never leave you nor forsake you." That is our security as we live in the jungle of today.

CHAPTER 4

My Pet Leopard, Chota Raj, and Tragedy

Life was always interesting for each of us in our jungle home in North Lakhimpur, but I am sure that it was of more interest to me because I was growing up there, not knowing anything else in life. Our house, as I mentioned, was very rustic, but my mother made it *home*. I often think back and wonder how she put up with all of my different wild animal pets. I know she wasn't thrilled to share her home or surrounding area with them but she loved me enough to put up with this so that I might have a rich childhood. I had several monkeys, and they seemed to know that they were not my mother's favorite pets, but they were very special to me.

On one occasion some woodcutters came to our home about noon and wanted to see my father. All of this was because my father had been to many of the villages around the area. Many of these people had become Christians and highly respected my father.

When they saw him they said they had a present for his son. With that they pulled a little leopard cub out of a pouch that was hanging around the neck of one of the men. My father was surprised and very cautious. He knew that a leopard mother would follow the scent of the cub for many miles, and that would be very dangerous for us. They assured him that they had killed the mother because she tried to kill one of them.

After talking with them for some time and talking with my mother about this new pet, he agreed to take the cub and give it to me. My mother was not too sure it would be a good idea to have the cub around the house, especially when it grew up! She did agree, though, and they called me and presented this little leopard to me. To say the least, this little jungle boy was thrilled beyond anything that could be placed on this paper.

I had to promise to help feed him and keep his place clean. This I did heartily, but, of course, the night-time feedings were done by my father. I will have to say that he was quite a father for the adventurer son of his. This expression of love to me and for me taught me many lessons in the life that I have lived since then.

We gave the little leopard the name of Chota Raj, which means Little King. He could not have had the name of Raja, which means King, because the royal Bengal tiger of India was the only one that could have that title. The leopard was much smaller; therefore we named him Little King. This is how life began with my newest pet from the jungle.

Everything went well for the first month or so. His eyes began to open, and he started running around the house and seemed to get into a lot of trouble. As he got a little older he would chase my monkey around and really seemed to know that one day he could have him for lunch!

As the days went by my father felt that the danger from my little leopard's mother was on his mind more and more. What if indeed she had survived and the story told him by the men just might not have been true. Dad had some very uneasy feelings.   This became more on his mind as he talked to many of the village people and they were warning him about the little leopard. This was a very real threat if, indeed, the mother had survived, because we lived just about 100 feet from the start of the jungle. The threat from the jungle had many faces and it always kept my mother concerned. Life went on for all of us until one night my father got up to check Little Raj because he was so very restless and crying very strangely.

As I have already told you, our house was built upon stilts made from trees cut from the jungle. The house stood about seven feet above the ground and had a cook house, or kitchen, on the same level, but separated by a breezeway that connected the two buildings. There was a screen door that had been reinforced to protect from jungle animals, yet the breeze could come through and one could look out.

As my father checked on Little Raj, his flashlight revealed the fiery, yellow eyes of a big leopard staring at him from the breezeway between the kitchen and the house. By this time Little Raj was going wild, crying loudly, and the leopard outside the screen door was starting to growl. My father shouted at the leopard outside the door and grabbed a big stick and struck the wall to scare it away, and finally it left the landing and jumped down. By this time everybody in the house was awake, and the helpers came because they had heard my father shout and came to see what had happened. There was much discussion as to the identity of this leopard. The conclusion by the leaders of the village was that the leopard in the breezeway was indeed the mother of the cub, otherwise it would not have come to where the little cub was. She had followed the scent of the little leopard to our house. The thing that confused everybody was the fact that it had taken so long for her to find the cub.

The next day all the people from our village heard what had happened the night before and came by to talk with my father and give him advice about what to do with my little leopard. Of course, everybody had the right idea as to what to do. Turning the cub loose into the jungle to find its mother sounded like a good idea, except for the fact that human scent was all over the cub. When the mother would smell that, she would not take the cub back but would reject it—or even kill it!

To do nothing and still keep the cub put *me* in danger because the mother now knew where the cub was, and even though she would not take it back she hadn't gotten close to it to smell the human sent. She would still come around to check out the cub. The thought from the village elders was that my life would be in great danger because our house was so close to the jungle, and playing there I could face the danger of the mother coming back to snatch me out of the yard and kill me. The thought of sending him to the zoo was out of the question because we were so very far from the zoo in Calcutta. A great thought but it couldn't be done.

This is the tragic part of this story: the decision was made to kill the cub and put the body into the jungle next to our house. This way the mother would find the cub, know that it was dead and would go back into the deep jungle from where she had evidently come.

This is the story of my pet, Little Raj, who gave me so much fun until the day that his mother came looking for her little cub. My life of fun was cut short, but was basically saved by the actions of a wise and loving father and the village elders.

I have often thought of this time in my life as an example of a loving heavenly Father who protects me as my earthly father protected me in this time in my life.

Remember that everything in life does not always turn out the way you think it should. This was certainly the case with my Chota Raj and his life, but there was something good that came out of the experience of his short life. First, I didn't get killed by his mother when I was playing in the yard. Secondly, my father took steps to make our house more secure from the jungle animals for all of us as a result of this episode. So you see, even in this experience there was a purpose.

I have often thought of this time in my life when I didn't have any idea of how to protect myself from the things that could harm me. All I could think of was the fun I was having with my little leopard. Remember that in our lives we often do not know how to protect ourselves because we simply do not know the future. This is the time to commit yourself to the Lord Jesus and His care, trusting that He will care for us.

We are reminded of the Scripture where it says, "Casting all your care on Him for He cares for you." So live today, *trusting* Him totally, for He cares for your life.

Remember, too, that the Lord will give His best to those who leave the choice to Him.

CHAPTER 5

The Charging Elephant that Saw an Angel!

I have mentioned that my father would go on tour many times through the year. He would always take some of his men whom he was training to become preachers and evangelists for the area. He was always teaching someone, as I remember. As I look back at his life, this was the reason he was able to touch so much of India with the good news of salvation. He trained many, and because of that there are thousands of churches in that part of India today.

We all stood in the yard and waved to them as they drove off into the jungle area. He was gone for a number of weeks and finally returned. After some time he gathered the family and told us of an experience he had on this last trip.

He said that they had taken the car to a certain village where the car road ended. From there on it was a path only passable by foot or oxcart. By this time he said that it was getting rather late in the afternoon, and by morning he had to be in the village where the meetings were to be held. He went to the head man of the village and asked if he could hire an oxcart for the trip through the jungle. Dad knew that it would take most of the night to get to the place for his ministry the next day.

The head man said, "No, it would not be possible to go through the jungle at night because of the wild elephants that are there." My father insisted that he had to get there for the next morning. He noticed several oxcart drivers listening closely so Dad said, "I will give you double the money that would be normal if someone will go."

One man was interested and said he would go on these conditions: two men would go before the cart and two behind the oxcart, and one on each side, and they would need to have fire torches burning in their hands through the deep jungle. He said he would have to go and give a sacrifice to his god before he would go, and so he did. My father agreed on a price, and they started out from the village late in the afternoon. They had walked for some time when they decided that they needed to stop and make some tea. Tea is the fuel to keep one going in the heat of the tropics.

Before they started out once again my father prayed, asking the Lord Jesus for protection for them and the oxcart driver. In his prayer Dad gave the message of salvation, and this was the first time that the oxcart driver had heard about a God who cared for people and wanted them in heaven with Him, of this I am sure. Dad's message about man's sinfulness and the pardon provided by the death of the Lord Jesus on the cross really seemed to touch this man's heart. All of this was a preparation for what was to transpire in the next number of hours. As they walked on he asked many questions, and Dad answered.

As they proceeded they had to make sure that the fire torches didn't go out, especially as they approached the deepest part of the jungle. Dad said that they had been walking for hours and everybody was walking just like a robot when, all of a sudden, there was a trumpeting coming from the jungle to the right of the path. Then there was a crashing as the trees were being knocked down by the force of the charging elephant. Dad said that the ox-cart driver started screaming to his god to help him. Dad said he prayed out loud, "Lord God, You are more powerful than this elephant, and You can protect us."

Then all of a sudden the wild elephant crashed into the opening in front of them! Dad said all were frightened, but somehow he felt very confident that the Lord would stop this charging elephant. He started to come at them on his second charge, but all of a sudden he stopped and raised his trunk as if he had seen something that terrified him. Then he trumpeted in terror and he turned and fled back into the jungle from where he had come! They heard the terrified trumpeting of the bull elephant as he ran from them. The oxcart driver came over to my father, fell at his feet and said that Dad's God was more powerful than his, because he had never seen an elephant stop after starting on his second charge! Many times they will stop on their first charge, trying to bluff their intruders, but *never* on the second.

Dad said that he was sure the elephant had seen more than just them and their torches because of the way the animal shrieked as he fled into the jungle. He felt that the Lord had sent an angel to stand before the elephant to protect them. Finally they arrived in the village where many were waiting. After getting refreshed a bit my father and the men with him started the meetings.

The oxcart driver said he wanted to know more about the God who could turn back a charging elephant. After talking to him, he decided to stay in the village and learn more about the God that cared about people. Dad said he stayed and learned about the Lord Jesus, deciding to live in the village till he, too, could become a Christian.

This was just one more example to me that the God my father and mother served was indeed the God of the Bible—and I wanted to make sure that *I* knew Him too as I lived my life.

It is interesting that in our country we don't seem to have this type of experience, but wait a moment. What of all the things that could have happened to you in your daily life, and think of how you may have been protected without knowing it. Remember, when you belong to the Lord Jesus you are *His* property and He wants you to fulfill *His* purpose in life. Your life one day will be revealed to you by the Lord, and you will see that He protected you every bit as much. Trust the Lord Jesus with your life and live to the fullest.

In our day there are many things that can destroy your life, the awful things that are there to tempt you. Yielding to them will slowly destroy the life that the Lord has given you. Be sure that you know Him and daily live so that He might guide you and protect you on your life's pathway.

CHAPTER 6

A Leopard Under the Cot

After arriving in our jungle home and making the house livable, my parents settled into the life of pioneer missionaries. Often my father would take trips into the most remote jungle areas, visiting the many villages, checking on the few Christians in the area and would also go to villages showing his pictures on the life of Christ. He became known as the *noxa walla* or Picture Man. He had taken a five gallon can and made a projector out of it. There was no electricity so his source of light had to be a specially designed kerosene light. He would also take a sheet and stretch it up over some bamboo poles and show the pictures in the village square at night. Often he would be gone from home for many weeks at a time. In these jungles there were elephants, tigers, leopards and many snakes which made it a very dangerous place to be. This would make for tremendous and fascinating evenings of story telling when he came home. We didn't have television, but the jungle had its own entertainment.

On one occasion he told about going to a village on the border of the kingdom of Bhutan where there were a few Christians. He said that it was a wild place deep in the jungle. To get to the village they took the car to where the road ended and then walked for several days through the jungle. They had a tent and bed rolls in which to sleep. For cooking and protection from the animals in the jungle they had to gather a lot of firewood. Going to these places they always tried to stay in the safest place they could find. There were often encounters with the residents of the jungle as they traveled.

They finally arrived at the village and were met by the whole population, even the chief! All of the people were excited to have him come, probably the first white man many had ever seen. Dad had some of his evangelists with him and together they made a complete team to reach the villages in the area. He wanted to teach them that one day they could do this without him. My father was forever the teacher, and that never changed all through his life—and, I might say, mine. Upon arrival the chief took him over to his hut for tea and formal greetings from the village elders. After this time of getting acquainted the chief took my father to a new house built in his honor, the custom in that area when a person of great importance came to visit a village. What a special honor! My father was interested not to offend the chief and village elders. That time of the year was very hot, and the humidity was extreme. The house was built of bamboo and then they plastered all the walls of the house with a mixture of water, mud and cow manure. There were no windows in the whole house, and the plaster had not totally dried so there was quite an odor. My father said he almost passed out from the odor and told his men that it would be very difficult for him to stay inside the house, but he didn't want to offend the village leaders. He asked the men who had come with him to help, and they came up with a plan. They told the chief that the white man was from a cold country and that he could not sleep where there was no air. The chief said he understood, but he was very concerned with the thought of Dad being exposed to leopards that could harm him. They would often come into the village at night and kill a calf or anything else that was out in the open.

They then presented their plan that pleased the chief by saying they would place a kerosene lamp on either side of the opening into the house and place a cot in between. Then they would sleep in the house and my father would sleep just outside the door. This pleased everyone.

After the agreement with the chief, he and the village elders invited my father and his men to share their evening meal. As they sat on the ground surrounded by the village elders, they realized that the entire village was surrounding them and watching them eat their spicy rice and curry meal. The chief way very concerned that my father was satisfied with what he had presented him. My father assured him that the meal was the *best* it could have been.

After the meal plans were made for the evening meeting which was to be held in the village center. The new Christians were eager to learn more about their faith and to share it with the whole village. The evangelists wanted the villagers to hear the good news that there was a God who loved them and made it possible for them to have their sins forgiven through the pardon on the cross by the Lord Jesus Christ. My father showed pictures on the life of Christ and the plan for eternal salvation.

The village people listened eagerly, and many that night wanted to accept the pardon for their sin and be assured of heaven. The tremendous thing that happened that night was that the village chief came to my father and asked if he could have the pardon of God for his sin, because he had been very wicked. After showing him from the Scripture how the Lord Jesus would forgive all that would come to Him in repentance, he fell on his knees and accepted his new-found Redeemer. This was the start of that whole village becoming a Christian village in time to come.

Before they all returned to their huts, my father said that God would take care of them and protect them in the midst of this wild jungle area. They bade each other a good night, and my father and his men went to the place prepared for them.

As his men went into the house, my father got onto his cot and tucked in his mosquito net and they all said goodnight to each other. My father said he thought of the statements of the chief about the leopards and loose calves, but finally he drifted off to sleep. About midnight something bumped his bed and awakened him. He was fully wide awake immediately, but didn't know what had bumped his cot. He thought that maybe a calf was loose. He was just about to call the people of a nearby hut to take the calf in when the dog under his bed gave an awful yelp; he came to full consciousness, realizing he was looking at a leopard next to his cot! The next thing he saw was the leopard leaping away with the dog in his mouth! He said he trembled for a few minutes when he realized just what had happened and was almost ready to go into the house. Then he realized he had told the villagers that God would protect them, so he knew that he would have to stay outside on the cot if his message was to be strong and believed by the villagers. He said he prayed and asked the Lord for help and then he said, "Believe it or not, I went to sleep!"

What a story! But this was just one of the many stories that became a part of my life while I lived in the jungles of my home in North East India.

It amazed me to realize that my father exposed himself to many dangers that could have taken his life. I understand that my mother took courage from the Lord as she spent many days and weeks alone when her husband was gone into the jungles with no contact possible. This is a story of true commitment to the Lord and to their desire to fulfill their part in carrying out the great commission of the Lord Jesus Christ. What an example for me and, might I say, for many others.

As I have reflected on this experience in the years that have followed, some indelible impressions have been left on my mind. The price of being God's servant is often not easy, but the results are fulfilling. This was certainly the case in the lives of my father and mother. Maybe this story will help each evaluate and then do what the Lord desires of us.

$$\underline{\text{ঔ}}$$

CHAPTER 7

The Fighting Elephants

One vivid memory that I have from my boyhood in India took place in Assam, in North East India. For the first several years my father and mother worked with the tribal people of that area. My father often would go into the interior of the area to hold meetings for pastors and the Christians.

On one occasion he wanted the entire family to go because there was a new road to the village in which the meetings were to be held. Because of that fact he felt it would be a good experience for the family and for the people of the area to see them all.

Preparations were made; the bedrolls were packed onto our 1929 Model A Ford. The food was put into containers to be eaten on the schedule my mother had made according to the spoiling time for the food, because we did not have any ice for coolers or anything that could be called a cooler.

The day came when we all got into the car: my father and mother, my two sisters and I and our cook, Medhavilo, and we left for the meetings. We were quite a sight with bedding rolls and cots on the top of the car, gas cans on the back bumper and two extra tires tied to the spare. You have to know that there were no gas stations or places to repair cars so all the extras had to be taken along.

This trip was to take us two full days. The first day went well, and we stopped at a *dhak bungalow*, a place built for British government officials. My father had gotten permission to stay in these bungalows from the British government officials who controlled the area. Remember, during these days India was a very proud member of the British Empire.

Early the next morning we left for the trip through the thickest part of the jungle, then on to the village. Everything went well as the miles passed. Toward early afternoon we started through the wildest part of the jungle. My younger sisters and I were excitedly looking for any animals we might see. We started to see monkeys everywhere, and then a jackal crossed the road. After a bit my father stopped, and we had a great picnic.

My father thought we would have no trouble getting to the village by four or five o'clock in the afternoon. As we were going along, all of a sudden there was quite a noise, and we looked back and saw that the battery had fallen out of the car and had broken! We were stopped in the middle of the deep jungle, and there was nobody on the road who could help us. Finally the decision was made that my father and our cook would walk to the next village to see if they might be able to get some help. I could never tell you enough about how much I admire my mother for the way she lived in those early pioneer days on the mission field. She had a tremendous love for the Lord Jesus and the mission she felt was so very necessary. I was about seven and my sisters were five and three, and here we were in the midst of one of the wildest jungles on the face of the earth and on a road that really was two parallel paths to fit the car tracks.

About an hour after my father and our cook disappeared down the road we heard some tremendous noise in the jungle to our right and some trumpeting on our left. Instantly my mother got us all into the car. Then from the right side of our car about 50 to 75 yards in front of us a big bull elephant charged toward the noise on our left. Instantly another bull elephant came out of the jungle on our left and charged toward the other bull. The ground shook as they approached each other, each trumpeting and pushing over trees to let the other one know how very strong he was. Then they charged each other, wrapping their trunks around each other and trying to gore the other with their great tusks. My mother was pleading with the Lord to save our family. It was a terrifying time as these huge animals fought, trying to kill each other.

We sat there wondering what would happen next, not knowing if they would come close enough to crush the car in their fight against each other. They could have crushed the car like a match box if they came that way. On several occasions the fight came very close to us. As I turned away to watch the fight again, the biggest bull charged and hit the other bull with his trunk and knocked him down. He then started to jab the downed elephant with his tusks. The other elephant struggled to his feet and slowly backed off, then turned and ran into the jungle. The triumphant elephant trumpeted and slowly slipped from our view. We had witnessed one of the jungle's most vicious fights for supremacy among its giants!

I looked at my precious mother several times during this ordeal and saw her with her eyes closed, praying, tears flowing down her cheeks. I know that the Lord heard her prayer because we should not have survived.

Our hearts settled down and finally we started talking to each other, becoming quite concerned that my father and our cook had not returned yet. As the dusk settled on the jungle and our thoughts went from thinking of our *survival* to wondering if we would be spending the night *alone* in that now scary place. All of a sudden we screamed as we saw my father and our cook emerging from that part of the jungle where the bull elephant had first come from. Mother ran and embraced Dad and cried. She then told him of our ordeal with the elephants. Dad and Medhavilo had their own miracle story about the battery they had been able to get from a tea planter about 20 miles from where we were stranded. That is, of course, another story.

Dad put the battery into the car and we started again for the village, arriving there about eleven o'clock that night. We settled into our bamboo hut that had just been built for us. The next morning the meetings started as my father started speaking. This was one more event in the lives of pioneer missionaries and their missionary son.

Often times in life when we are doing what we feel we *should* be doing and we know that what we are doing is *right*, that problems seem to come up out of nowhere. This is the time to make sure that you have put your trust in the Lord Jesus and then allow Him to give you the strength to face that which you did not expect to happen. In the midst of life we are often confronted with what we cannot handle. This is the time to tell the Lord that you cannot do what is necessary to be done, but you are going to trust Him. This type of experience is what will make you stronger than you would be without it. I know that our experience made my mother stronger in that pioneer situation. I know seeing my mother pray and trust the Lord for her little family has made me stronger to this day. I know that often I realize I *cannot*, then I am reminded that He (God) *can*, and because of this knowledge I by His strength *will*. There will be days when it seems that the evil one is about to trample you with his power, and there is absolutely nothing you can do. It is at a time like this you hear the Lord Jesus say, "I am with you always; be not afraid."

෯

CHAPTER 8

Tiger on the Pathway

As you know, my home was in the midst of a very large jungle, and my father often would be gone for a week or longer at a time. He would go to villages to tell the people that the way to heaven was through trusting the Lord Jesus. This was quite a new thought to so many who lived deep in this jungle area. He would tell them that they could not do enough good works to get to heaven, and that God was not an angry God who desired to punish and destroy them. Most of them believed that they had to do something to appease their gods. They were fearful because they felt that their god was angry at them and wanted to hurt them or destroy them. My father told them that God loved them and paid the penalty for their sins on the cross. He died that they might live with Him in eternity. Now to hear that this God loved them and was willing to forgive them was absolutely an unbelievable thought. It was amazing to see how many of these people put their trust in the Lord Jesus, and they were thrilled to know that they would now go to heaven when they died. This was the reason my father and mother had given their lives to be carriers of the good news of heaven, and now they were seeing the results. Soon there were many Christians in the area, and churches sprang up all over. My father would go to help them and encourage them as new believers.

It was when he was getting ready to go on one of these trips that I asked him if I could go along. He told me that if I would get my school work done ahead for the next two weeks, then I could go. My mother was teaching me in the Calvert's system during that time. I worked very hard doing two days of lessons in one and did exactly what Dad had told me to do—and now I was ready and excited to go.

The day came for us to depart. The 1929 Model A was packed, and several of dad's men who were evangelists were going on this trip. We waved to my mother and sisters and were ready for what was ahead in the next days. The road was very rough and muddy, but we went along very rapidly for jungle transportation. We finally came to the end of the road for cars, so we left the car in the village. My father hired an ox cart to take the things that would be needed for the meetings, like his special projector to show the pictures on the life of Christ. It was about noon so we had something to eat, and drank some tea and left the village. We walked for many hours through the jungle, but sometimes I would go back and sit on the oxcart until it became unbearable to ride any more.

Dad and I were walking quite a distance ahead of the oxcart and the other men. May I say I didn't realize how very special these times really were, not knowing that it would not be long until I would be separated from him for many years. During these times he would talk of my relationship with the Lord Jesus and ask how much time I was spending reading the Bible and if it was meaningful to me. These were good times in my young life. Going to boarding school during the days of World War II would be the thing that would bring separation to our lives. We talked about many things as we walked along, but soon it seemed we had walked for an eternity. In reality, it was about 5:30 p.m. It was hot, and the path was dusty, and I became a little like a robot, just putting one foot in front of another.

The air started to take on the coolness of the jungle as the hours moved on. All of a sudden as we were looking down the path, a movement caught my dad's eyes and mine too. There out of the jungle came a tiger! Carefully my father grabbed my arm and said to stand still and not to move and not be scared. That was a hard thing to do, that's for sure, especially looking at that big tiger that was now walking down the path toward us!

The rest of the party was a long way back so there was nothing they could do for us. It seemed that the tiger walked forever toward us. One thing you do not want to do is turn and run. The tiger will then start running after you because you look like dinner to him! There wasn't much we could do but stand our ground and pray. Dad squeezed my arm very hard. I think this was what he did to have me think of the pain rather than the approaching tiger. That tiger looked huge—and he *was*! When you are on the same level as a royal Bengal tiger he is big! The tiger kept coming closer and closer, sniffing the air and looking us over very carefully. We could smell the tiger as he was upwind from us, and it is a smell I haven't forgotten to this day!

He carefully looked us over; we stood so very still and again prayed that the Lord Jesus would help us. All of a sudden he looked right at us and then, he slowly slipped off into the jungle. We both were trembling, and my dad took me in his arms and again he prayed and thanked the Lord for His divine protection.

Shortly after the tiger went into the jungle, the ox cart and the other men came up to us. They said they would like to stop for a while, but my father insisted that we go on from there! As we were walking he told them what had happened. After hearing this they didn't want to stop till we got to the next village where we spent the night. The people in the village asked my father if we had seen a tiger. He then told them the story and they told him that they had been frightened by this tiger a number of times in the last few days. My father told them how his God had protected us on the path that day. The people of the village wanted to hear more about his God. Because of their desire, Dad and his men had a meeting that night in the center of the village. Today there is a church there, and many of the people of the village have become Christians. So I guess that the Lord even used a tiger on the path for His purpose.

The next day we went on to the place where the meetings were to be held. We were greeted warmly by the village chief and the leaders of the village. Yes, my father had a wonderful week of telling these people about the Lord Jesus. When I relive this experience I am reminded that nothing in life is an accident for the one who is related to the Lord Jesus. He has a plan and purpose for everything that happens to us. This is what has impressed itself on me and my life, and I desire to let every experience be used consciously or unconsciously for the plan and purpose of the Lord.

One of the lessons that I learned was how much like the Lord my father was during this experience as he did his best to help me do the right thing in this circumstance with the tiger. He kept my attention on him instead of the tiger as he squeezed my arm, and he spoke reassuringly to me in the presence of danger and then hugged me and prayed when the danger was over. *What a Dad* who reminded me of *what a God!* I might say that life lived for the Lord does not have to be boring.

This was another experience in my life as a boy and, as I have thought back on those days, it really was QUITE A LIFE!

CHAPTER 9

Sunrise and the Golden Tigers

The heat was unbearable in the jungle during the hot season, and all of us kids were suffering from prickly heat over much of our bodies. At tea time one afternoon my father announced that we would be going up to the mountains for a holiday in the cool climate. There was a shout from all of us because we loved being in the hills in the cool, and we could even have a fire in the fireplace in the evenings.

We packed up the car and drove to the Brahmaputra River where we took the ferry down the river to Guwahati. There we got on a *lorry* (truck) that would take us up to Kohima and then on to Khangpopi. The trip was really fun because we rode on top of bags of different supplies that were to go up the mountain for the merchants in the towns along the way.

These mountain roads were really treacherous as they had been cut out of the side of the mountain and were only wide enough for one-way traffic. The cliff on which the road hung was absolutely awesome. Looking over the side you looked down thousands of feet and saw a little river at the very bottom. It was quite a trip up this one-way road that often had landslides which would block it, and one would have to get out and walk to the other side of the slide and get in another truck. All the merchandise had to be transported by coolies over the slide to the other truck. My mother would tell us to be careful, but to us this was incredible fun. If all would go well the traffic on the way down the mountain used the road from 6:00 in the morning till 12:00 noon. Then the traffic that was at the bottom would start up the mountain, using it between 12:00 noon and 6:00 p.m.

We finally got settled again on top of the bags of cotton and other things, and our trip was again under way. We placed ourselves so we had an excellent view out of the open sides of the *lorry*. My mother sat in the front seat with my littlest sister, Joanne, who always got car sick. My sister Mary loved being with me on the cotton bags in the back of the truck. We wound up the side of the mountain, grinding away in the lower gears. Often we would stop to let us out to stretch and run around a bit and this became our bathroom break, too. Not much was private to be sure, but that is how it was in those years. Then we'd get back into the truck finally reaching Kohima, a hill village, around 6:00 in the evening.

We stayed that night with missionary friends of ours and loved being in the cool. The next morning we loaded ourselves on another truck to Khangpopi. After traveling most of the day on the winding mountain roads, we finally saw the mission station come into view. Our hearts raced because we would be together with friends whom we had not seen for a long time. My best friend, John Ahlquist, was standing there waiting for me. His father was a missionary doctor who would team up with my father for work in the villages near their mission station.

We arrived with excitement as we jumped out of the truck and into the arms of our friends. They had all been standing there waiting for us to come, and now we were finally together. We were thrilled to be a part of their mission station for the next month.

As we entered the house we were shown where we were going to stay. Our accommodations were a bedding roll on the floor, and we made sure that we were as close together as we could be. There's no relationship like that of being a missionary kid on a foreign field, something that says that you belong together as nothing else I have experienced in my lifetime.

We had a wonderful time that evening, telling each other of all the things that had taken place in our lives the past year since we had last been together. Slowly we went to our places to sleep and slept extremely well because of the cool weather. We even had to put on some blankets! It was heavenly sleep!

The next morning we had a great breakfast of pancakes that Dr. Ahlquist, Uncle Doc to us, had made. He would write our names on the pancake and then give it to each one of us. What fun this was; I was sure these days were going to be wonderful.

Days came and went and many things happened, including my being stung by the biggest black wasp I had ever seen. This sting took place as my friend John and I went for a hike into the mountains not far from their home. As we hiked along we spotted a tremendous wasp hive. It was fully five to six feet in length. We watched for a while, and then my friend took a rock and threw it at the hive. All of a sudden, here came hundreds of angry wasps! We both started running and got away from most of them, but all of a sudden one flew right toward me and stung me in the back of my head. The wasp was about one and a half inches in length and was black and orange. I killed it, but not until it had done some damage to me. By the time we got home my head was throbbing like nothing I had ever experienced before. Uncle Doc took a look at me, gave me an injection, placed ice on my head and bound it tightly. I suffered for several days and was lectured to by the nationals and my father. Don't ever throw rocks at wasp hives if you don't want to be stung. I learned my lesson even though I didn't throw the stone that created the problem.

Two days later Uncle Doc took some of the men hunting for wild boar because they wanted to give a treat to the people of the compound. I asked if I could go along and was told to get my friend John and come. Wow, what a time it was for us all as we hunted. All of a sudden after going about two miles into the jungle we came across the rutting of wild boar. After that there was quite a commotion in the jungle and, before I knew what was going on, a shot rang out and then a squealing! Then there was victorious shouting that signified a wild boar had been shot and there would be a feast on the compound that night. And there was! Uncle Doc was the one who shot the wild boar, and everybody began jumping and shouting as they carried the boar back to the compound. Even though I was just one of the party that went hunting, I was received as if I had a part in the shooting of the wild boar when we came into the village with the kill.

While I was there I became acquainted with many new friends who told me of many things they had seen in the mountain jungles, including tigers. I have always loved tigers since I had my pet tiger named Raja, which means King. When they would talk of tigers I would often ask where they were and they would answer, "Over the mountain." My heart was set on getting to see one somewhere in that area.

One morning I woke up very early when it was still dark, and I left the house without anyone knowing I was gone. I left the compound area and took the path toward the mountain that I thought my new friends were talking about. I knew this was not a very good thing to do because it is very dangerous to go out into this type of jungle alone, but I wanted to see a tiger so badly I really didn't think about it too long and just kept on going. As I walked along I came across some of the jungle animals: a jackal, a wild pig, jungle fowl, some big bats returning from a night of hunting, and a cobra about four feet long. Yes, this was my kind of jungle, I thought, as I walked along. As I continued I came to an opening on the side of the mountain where the trees had been logged off by the tribesmen. As I looked up on the mountain side it was covered by tall grass which grew about two or three feet high. The sun was just breaking over the mountain as I was moving along. All of a sudden I saw movement close to the top of the mountain, and I froze because up there in front of me was the most beautiful sight I had ever seen. There, standing before me, about 100 yards away, was a royal Bengal tiger with the sun glistening off her coat. All of a sudden I realized she was not alone. She had two cubs standing by her side. I was absolutely fascinated beyond words. They looked as if they were made of pure gold because of the way the sun was shining on them. As I was standing there looking at them, all of a sudden I saw the mother tiger's tail start to twitch back and forth and I realized that she was getting my scent as the slight air blew her way, and I realized that I was in real danger. I slowly moved backward toward the jungle I had just come out of. I kept my eyes on the tigers, trying to move so that the breeze would not carry my scent toward her and her two cubs. This was very exciting and very dangerous, but on the other hand, I was loving every precious moment of this time because of what I was seeing. At the same time I realized that I had better get myself out of sight and smell. I left those beautiful creatures that the Lord God had created, and I felt as though I had seen something that I would never see again in my lifetime, a sight out of this world. Yes, I felt that I had a glimpse of something totally unreal—and it *was!* I stopped right there and said thank you to the Lord who I believe allowed me the privilege of seeing these tigers of gold.

I did move rather quickly back to the compound and got there just as everybody was awakening. What a morning I had had; what a memory to pass on to you. Oh, yes, the adults did ask me how I enjoyed the night. I said it was wonderful, and the morning was wonderful, too. I didn't tell anyone but my friend Johnny, and I swore him to secrecy! He was very troubled with me that I had not asked him to go along, but then I would never have seen the tigers, because he always had trouble keeping quiet when we were in the jungle. I did tell my folks about this, but it was about four years later when the timing was perfect.

The next time you see a tiger in the zoo or some other place, try to imagine that tiger standing on a mountainside with the sun glistening off of its beautiful coat—and remember you heard that from an old missionary kid!

I want you to know, too, that the Lord gives us some special experiences in life, and we need to make sure that we realize they are a gift from Him. The Bible says that every good and perfect gift comes to us from the Lord. As you live, try and make sure that you look at every experience as a unique gift given to us to make our lives special. Let's make sure that we don't just live life existing, but live to the fullest remembering that the Lord wants us to have the very best *in* life and *out of* our lives.

So many times I meet people who don't seem to be alive to anything around them. I think that it is often our fault if we don't have some thrilling experiences to speak of. It is often because we are not looking for them in the place where we live. I would suggest that you look around and examine your life, expecting something special. This is too often the case when we think of the Lord Jesus, but our lives do not respond to Him in a special way. It is because we are not looking to the Word of God to examine the Lord Jesus in the light of living a fulfilling life. As we walk with the Lord Jesus in our daily life we need to realize that He desires that we live an abundant life. We need to live life *that* way and thank Him for His touch in our life as we live it excitedly *with* and *for* Him.

CHAPTER 10

A Tiger and the Wrong End of a Gun!

Every year one of the highlights of the lives of all missionary kids was the annual conference. This was a time when the missionaries would get together from all over North East India. They would give their reports of the last year and then they would make plans for the year to come. This was not the reason we loved the conference time, but, rather, it was the only time many of us would see another white child! One of the problems was the fact that often we could not communicate with each other because we only knew the languages of our area and didn't speak English. Believe me, we learned from each other very quickly. We all understood English, but would not speak it because no other child in our areas spoke English.

One of the things we as kids loved was when the adults would have a skit night. We would see those who were respected by all the nationals and by the missionaries as their leaders do crazy things in some sort of a skit. I remember one had to do with a time machine when something or someone would go into one side of the machine and come out the other end changed! I was shocked when my father, whom I felt was so serious, entered the time machine dressed in a suit and then came out the other end dressed in a diaper. I didn't know if I should laugh or not, but when everybody else was laughing I did too. That was a side of my father I had not seen before, but that was one of the special things of our yearly conference that I shall always remember.

Every year we would have story time for the children of the

missionaries when the adults would come and tell us stories of their experiences on the frontier. It wasn't long before we knew who could tell a good story and who couldn't. Those were enjoyable times for each of us as we related to the whole missionary family. This created a bond between the adult missionaries and the children, and they really became our uncles and aunties. This became our real family and is one of the reasons why missionary life is so special to missionary kids.

I remember one particular year when we were in Sadiya, and one of the oldest missionaries, Uncle Swanson, got us together to tell some stories. He started out telling us how he was going to a particular village in his old Model T Ford. As he was driving along he spotted a tiger off to the left of the rugged, rutty road. He said the tiger was acting very strangely, especially because he did not run away.   He stopped the car and waited to see what the tiger was going to do when all of a sudden it started running toward him. He grabbed his rifle and slowly got out of the car and faced the oncoming tiger. He carefully kept his eye on the tiger.   All of a sudden the tiger continued moving slowly toward him, growling loudly as he came. He put his rifle to his shoulder and fired. This tiger hardly flinched and kept charging toward him. His rifle jammed, and he was now facing certain death from the tiger. Thinking quickly, he turned his rifle around and jammed the butt end of the rifle into the open, snarling mouth of the angry tiger. The tiger swiped him with his front paws first of all, tearing into his leg. Then again he was hit by the other paw which tore into his side. The thought of death was on his mind, and he prayed, asking the Lord Jesus to help him in this life-and-death fight. All of a sudden he realized he was very close to the side of his car. In a miraculous moment he reached into the car and grabbed his heavy caliber revolver and shot the tiger with all five shots. The tiger died by the side of the car, touching Uncle Swanson's feet. He said that despite bleeding quite badly, he instantly fell to his knees and thanked the Lord for saving his life. By this time some villagers came around and seeing the dead tiger told him of a crazy tiger that had been giving them problems. Uncle then decided that the tiger must have had some sort of disease so he asked them to burn the carcass so there would not be any sickness from it. They did and thanked him very much for killing the tiger. After this he got into his car and went to the mission hospital where he spent several weeks getting his infected wounds cared for. The infection from the claws of a big cat is very hard to get rid of, but the mission hospital had a lot of experience in treating wounds from leopards, tigers and many other jungle animals. How thankful all of the people on mission fields are for missionary hospitals.

When he was through with the story all of us said that was not possible; it couldn't be true. He said, "Wait here a minute," as he went up the stairs to the verandah of his home. He was gone for a few moments and reappeared with an old rifle in his hands. Our eyes were all glued to the gun as he came to us. He then showed us the butt end of the gun that had been shattered by the teeth of the tiger! Then he said, "Now do you believe me?" There was a cheer from us all, and we said we *did* believe!

He then said that the Lord Jesus was the One who had protected him and gave him the chance to get hold of the revolver. He became our favorite missionary Grandpa, and from that time on we would always have him tell us this story. Then we would go into his bungalow and look at that old rifle with the split stock (butt end) that had been splintered by the teeth of the tiger!

This is just another story from the frontier of the mission field where I was raised. This became part of who I am today. I think that Uncle Swanson's giving the Lord the credit for his life helped me as a young boy to think of the Lord Jesus as the One who cared for us and protected us in some very difficult times.

This story is one that will give you an insight into the life of missionary kids on the mission field and the family that the Lord gives us to help when their own is on the other side of the world. I want you to make sure that you do your best to be family to someone that maybe doesn't have much of one. When we belong to the Lord Jesus we belong to His family, and it is our responsibility to help them feel they belong to that great family of the Lord. It is our privilege to help introduce them to Him.

CHAPTER 11

To Wake a Sleeping Tiger

During my boyhood I grew up with many friends who were all Indian. It was interesting that we all had to learn four different languages in order to be able to communicate with all the different people that we had to deal with in the village. So I learned four different languages before I would speak English.

I remember the first time I realized I was different from all my friends, when they started to call me "Bogha Bandore" which means "White Monkey." I was greatly troubled and went to my father telling him my problem and what they were calling me. He stopped for a moment and said, "So they are brown monkeys; just go and play." That was all the concern he gave it so I did just that, but from that time on I realized I was different than all the rest. It really didn't ever make any difference after that.

My best Indian friend was Bogha, whose name translated into English meant "white." He was named this because when he was born his skin was so much lighter than anyone else in his family. The lady that was helping his mother in delivery said, "bogha," and immediately his mother looked at him and said that would be his name. We were about the same age, and we did many things together, including going out into the jungle.

One morning when he came over I said to him, "Let's go into the jungle and see if we can hunt some birds with our slingshots." My father would not give me a gun at this time because he really was concerned that I might have a problem, and even get hurt or hurt someone else. We had made ourselves some very good slingshots that would kill birds and some smaller animals. We would take the birds we had killed and did a very crude job of taxidermy for our collection!

On this morning we decided to take a little food for lunch, and we took our slingshots with all the special "ammunition" we had. We had made clay balls and had let them bake in the sun for a number of days. They were made just the size for the pocket of our slingshots.

We walked into the jungle for a long time looking for a special type of bird that we wanted for our collection. As we walked along we saw many monkeys and birds, but not the type of bird we were looking for. As we continued walking on this animal trail we came to a place where the trail became a hole in the jungle which the animals used. I looked at Bogha and said, "Should we go in there?" He answered, "If you go, I will go." I didn't want him to think that I was afraid so I said, "Let's go, but let's be ready to retreat if we meet something we don't want to face." Rather dumb, as I look back, but we were just kids on an adventure.

I bent over quite a bit and started into the dense jungle. As I walked along all bent over I thought to myself, what if we run into an animal or snake, like a cobra that could kill us. We had been in the jungle many times, but never as deep as we were at this point. As we were going along, all of a sudden we heard a noise that sounded like thunder and I said to Boga, "It isn't even monsoon season and it's thundering." We walked along and all of a sudden the heavy jungle came to an end and the trail broke out into an opening that was covered with grass that stood about two to three feet tall. This grass was known as *tiger grass*, a kind of grass they used to thatch their houses.

We walked into it for a long time trying to see if we would see anything, when all of a sudden I saw the grass move ahead of us. I turned around and told Bogha to stay there; I would go up and shoot the bird that we had come to get. It was something like a pheasant in looks, very beautiful, and we wanted one very badly for our special collection.

The sun was rather hot and very bright, and in my mind I thought of the sound we had heard and wondered how we could have heard thunder when it was so bright and didn't look like a storm. As these thoughts were running through my mind I realized I was getting very close to where I had seen the grass move so I proceeded with care. I got close to the place where

I thought the special bird would be, and I got my slingshot ready. I carefully put out my foot and pulled back the grass to shoot when all of a sudden the head of a Royal Bengal Tiger lifted off the ground and looked right at me and gave a deep growl, as if to say, "What are you doing here?"

My heart almost stopped, and I backed up slowly till I had put some distance between the tiger and me. Then I started to run and ran right by Bogha, yelling that I had run into a tiger and he needed to run, too. We ran and ran as fast as we could possibly go. We were so scared we didn't remember that we had run through the tunnel part of the jungle! It seemed as if we ran forever, somehow not realizing how far we really were from home.

As we approached my home we ran directly to the wash shed in the back of our yard. Inside the shed we both were gasping for breath as we hung on to each other and trembled for a long time. When we finally got our breath Bogha asked me if the tiger had chased me. I said I didn't know. Obviously he had not because if he had chased me, I would have been his dinner! In the midst of all this we both looked at each other and thought we ought to pray and thank God that He took care of two dumb, adventurous boys. After a long time we decided it would be good if we didn't tell our parents, at least for a while. That night at the dinner table I had a hard time eating and my mother wondered what was wrong. Somehow I got through the evening without telling anything of the day's adventures.

Some of the things jungle boys get into are often kept in the heart for a long time because there was no desire to be put on restriction. By the way, I did tell my folks about this incident, though it was on the way back to the U.S.A. on board ship, a year or so after the fact!

Just remember, when you belong to the Lord Jesus He takes care of you even when you do some dumb things. So be careful and be smart, but always trust the Lord Jesus. I am reminded of the last part of the verse in Hebrews 13:5 which says, "I will never leave thee nor forsake thee." I am so glad it didn't say only when you are using your head. The Lord knows about our lives and how we act and react. He has a plan for our lives, and therefore we can trust Him to help us live our lives and protect us from ourselves.

What a wonderful thing it is to know that the one who loves us has this plan for us and we need to trust Him to care for us. I do not mean we should be careless, but we can know that everything that comes into our lives He will use to help us as we grow into adulthood. So remember to trust Him and walk with Him through your life, and He will produce His plan through you.

CHAPTER 12

The Woodcutter and the Tiger

My school work was getting boring, and I really wanted a change and something exciting. I went to my father's office and asked him if he was going to take another trip soon. He said, "Yes, in about two weeks." I asked if it would be at all possible for me to go along with him again the next time. He was a school man, to be sure, but he also knew that I needed something different at times. After waiting for a little time he said it might be possible if I would do well in my Calvert's school lessons and get ahead at least two weeks because that is how long he would be gone. I said I would, and tore into my school work with all my heart. And I did get ahead and was ready when Dad said he was going to leave.

The day came, and we packed the car with all the necessary food, clothes and bedding. Finally our cook and some of Dad's men, Dad and I were ready. We said goodbye to my mother and sisters, and we left. I was very excited as we went down the road toward the Naga Hills which held many intriguing memories for all of us.

We drove many hours to the foot of the mountains where the road ended and only a foot path led on up the mountains. These mountains were the home of the Naga people who were human head hunters—and they were fierce! The British, while they were in control in India, said of these people that they could never be tamed. They were barbarians of the first order. Into this wild area the missionaries went, and now there are many thousands who have become Christians.

Some of these areas still were head-hunting areas during my time there, even though it was against the law. But they did it anyway! Yes, I was very excited to go into this wild area and realize that it was the gospel of the Lord Jesus and salvation through His pardon that stopped head hunting in that area.

That night we camped by the car. We built a fire for cooking our food and then kept it going all night to keep the animals away. Our bedrolls were placed on the ground, a mosquito net was placed over us and we went to bed. I didn't sleep too much that night, hearing all the jungle noises of the wild elephants, the jackals, the hoot owls, a leopard and the roar of a large tiger. Finally I did drift off to sleep—and *suddenly* I was awakened by our cook bringing us some tea to start the morning! After breakfast we packed up and started up the mountain to go to the village of Meranakpu, where Dad was holding meetings for many of the villages around that area.

The walking was hard and very tiring, especially for some of the older men who were going with us. Hour after hour went by and finally we stopped to have some tea and sandwiches for lunch. After eating I had a lot of energy and went ahead of the group to explore, and then return to them to let them know that I was really all right. Later on toward dusk, when I thought it wouldn't be long before arriving at the village, I went on ahead quite a distance.

Mile after mile went by, and I was thinking that we would never arrive at the village. As I was going along rather slowly I felt a funny feeling come over me because I was a long way ahead of the others. All of a sudden, out of the jungle to my right came a thunderous roar! My heart almost stopped as I realized that it was coming from a tiger and, from the sound of the roar, he had to be big. I slowly turned around and started to go back to my dad and the group, going very carefully and slowly because I knew that one should never run from any animal that can kill you. Running triggers the instinct to chase and kill, thinking you would be their next dinner! The farther I got from the place where I heard the roar I began to move faster and then began to run. I ran faster and faster not thinking of anything except getting back to my father and the group coming up the mountain. I couldn't believe how far back they were, but finally I came around a bend and there they were! I walked over to my dad and told him what had happened. He took my hand and then told everybody that they had to all stick close together in case the tiger came looking for us. They all started to talk very loudly and sing very loudly. When we walked by the place where I heard the tiger, I walked on the other side of my father, but nothing happened!

Finally we reached the village and were met by a welcoming party and were immediately told of a woodcutter who had been killed by a tiger. When they told us where this happened I started to shake with fright because it was just about where I had heard the growl of the tiger. Evidently this all happened just about the time I was walking up the path. I felt very badly for the man that had been killed, but then I realized it could have just as easily been me! That evening after the meeting I talked to my father for quite a while about life and death. Dad told me that the Lord had a special job for me to do in life and that is why He spared me from the tiger that day.

This story is told so that every one of you might know that when you give your life into the keeping of the Lord Jesus, He will protect it until His plan for your life is fulfilled. That day I realized as never before that I was in the hands of a great God who had a plan for my life and I must be careful with my investment of it.

As I have looked back at this incident in my life I have come to realize that there is a plan for every life, even though we don't know at the time that there is one that is far greater than our own. He spares us or directs us in a way we do not know or necessarily understand, but trusting Him is the best thing we can do no matter how old we might be. Looking back at my life I have a great appreciation for the knowledge of protection and leading of our wonderful Savior, the Lord Jesus.

CHAPTER 13

Phantom in the Dark of Night

One of the wonderful things about living in a jungle area is that there are so many adventures that seem to be all around you as you grow up. This was the case in one of my very special memories from my childhood.

On our mission station there was a missionary who was well known for his ability in the jungle. His name was Dr. Brock, known to all of us missionary kids as Uncle Brock. The people of the area knew that if they had trouble with a man-eating tiger, leopard or panther, they could call on him to help them. He would help by killing the offending cat if it had killed some of their cattle or if they had someone attacked or killed in the village.

He became my hero in many ways as I frequently played with his son and often stayed with them overnight. At times like this he would tell of some of his experiences and I would be captivated by these accounts.

One day I heard he was going after a leopard that had killed a number of cattle and had attacked several people in a village a few miles away. They also mentioned to Uncle Brock that the leopard was the largest they had ever seen. On hearing this I went to see Uncle Brock and asked if it were possible for me to go along with him. His own son didn't have an adventurous desire in him so Uncle Brock was thrilled to have me ask if I could go along. He said it would be all right with him, but I would have to get the permission of my parents.

This turned out to be more difficult than I thought. I immediately went to see my father and asked him if it would be possible for me to go with Uncle Brock on the hunt for this killer leopard. He looked at me and said he thought it would be a great experience for me, but he thought my mother might not be so much in favor of it. Well, I left my father's office and looked for my mother in the back of the house. When I asked her, she was not in favor of this at all. I told her I would be perfectly safe because Uncle Brock was very careful and a very good hunter. She still didn't think this was a very good idea, but said she would talk to Dad about it and they would let me know. I really wanted to press for an answer but thought better of it. It seemed like an eternity before hearing back from them, but finally they called me into Dad's office and told me that I could go. I would have to promise not to do certain things and to make sure I obeyed Uncle Brock totally.

I couldn't wait to run over to Uncle Brock's bungalow and let him know that I could go along with him. He seemed to be happy and proceeded to give me instructions as to his rules for the hunt—and of course, I agreed totally because I wanted to go along with him so badly.

Plans were made and equipment was gathered and packed into his old Land Rover-type vehicle. Two days later we left the compound, with my mother looking very apprehensive as she waved goodbye. I was absolutely excited as we went down the road to the jungle cut off. There were five of us in the vehicle: Uncle Brock, his tracker, the cook, his helper and me. What a group we made for this adventure. We drove through the jungle on impossible roads with deep ruts, but the vehicle went through it all beautifully, even though it was very rough.

About noon we stopped in the middle of the jungle. The cook made us lunch with some good Assam tea, and we all felt better. After a number of hours we arrived at the village close to where the big cat had killed many of the village cattle and had attacked several people.

We were met by the village chief and elders, and Uncle Brock was treated like a king. We, too, all received the benefits of being in his party. They told everything about the big cat and said that they were very frightened of it and were fearful that one of them might be killed. They expressed their deep appreciation for the help and told him that the village tracker would go with us to show us where the last kill had been made.

This man knew the area where they had been confronted by the big cat, close to where he had made his last kill. They could not get over how unafraid of them the leopard seemed to be. They wanted Dr. Brock to come and kill the killer. As we traveled on we came to a river and were told that the kill was on the other side of the river and down quite a ways. We looked for a good area to set up camp on this side of the river where we would leave the vehicle. The tent was set up, and we gathered fire wood from the surrounding area and made preparations to cross the river. Before we left, Uncle went over to the vehicle and brought out a 22 caliber rifle. He said, "How would you like to use this?" All of this was so unexpected: that *I* would be a part of the hunt in a real way! It made my heart jump and my excitement factor go off the charts.

He carefully checked me out in handling the rifle. After setting up a target and seeing me hit close to the mark, he was satisfied. He watched how I handled the gun and felt that *I* would be safe with the weapon—as would all the *others* in the party!

The cook and the helper set up camp as the trackers and we went across the river in the little boat. It took two trips to get us over. As we walked toward the edge of the jungle, we could smell the odor of something dead.   When we had walked about a mile into the jungle, we came to the carcass of the cow which had been killed the day before. It was really smelly, and I had a hard time to keep from throwing up as I looked at the dead cow and smelled this decaying flesh.

The trackers spent about an hour looking for signs that the leopard had been in the area. They found the tracks and felt sure that the cat would return to the kill that evening. This was all very exciting to me as I envisioned being in the *machung* that night.

I watched as Uncle Brock and the tracker looked for a tree close by in which they could build a *machung*, a platform built in the tree where we could sit and observe the kill from a safe height. It wasn't long before they found a suitable tree, and the two trackers started cutting bamboo to create the platform. They did an incredible job, placing the platform about 15 feet up from the ground in the tree between three big branches. I looked around and found the tracks of the leopard, and I even climbed into the tree and sat on the *machung*.

By this time it was starting to get late in the afternoon when Uncle Brock said, "Let's go back to camp and eat dinner and then return to spend the night here, waiting for the cat to return to the kill."

We returned back to camp, crossing the river, where the cook had a nice fire going and a great meal prepared, along with a cup of tea. After we washed up at the river bank, we sat around the fire talking and eating. I was quite excited about the rest of the evening and night and was quite anxious to return to the *machung* and the kill.

About eight in the evening our tracker said it was time to go. I took my jacket and water and the gun I was given to use, and we left the camp. We again crossed the river and walked back to the tree in which the *machung* had been built. To be honest with you, I was really quite ready to get up into the *machung* because of the darkness and the noises from the evening jungle. The three of us climbed the tree into the *machung* and waited for the night to unfold. I was sure the leopard would return to his kill!

Uncle Brock instructed me about being quiet, and where I was to be if he would have the opportunity to get the shot at the leopard. I was so very excited—and my heart was telling me, as it boomed like a drum in my chest! The darkness settled very deeply, and the sounds of the jungle exploded in every direction. My thoughts and imagination were totally out of control. As the hours went by I calmed down, but my imagination didn't! I was sure I saw a python up above our *machung,* and I saw the shadow of a tiger walking below the tree we were in. We really did hear the sound of elephants trumpeting at each other, and we did hear a tiger roar, sending chilled blood through my veins.

What a night of anticipation it was as we waited for the leopard to return to the kill. Several hours into the night we heard the leopard roar, and again my heart started its own private concert on the drum in my chest. Again and again he roared and was coming closer to its kill and to us. Uncle Brock readied his rifle for the kill, but all of a sudden the leopard stopped coming toward us—at least for a while.

Several hours crept by as we sat in absolute silence. That silence was shattered by the eerie shriek of a peacock or the howl of a jackal, both being a reminder that we were in the depth of the jungle in the middle of the night. We sat waiting, and slowly I was overcome with a desire to sleep, but I knew that any minute the stealthy leopard could appear, and we had to be ready. But sleep was trying to capture me when all of a sudden I felt a tapping on my leg. It was Uncle Brock as he awakened me and pointed at a dark form bathed in the light of a cloud-covered moon. It was eerie as I had a feeling of something about to happen. And it did!

As I was looking into the fog that was starting to cover the jungle, I started to make out the form of a big cat silently moving toward its kill. That moment will be indelibly imprinted in my memory. I sat motionless, staring at this phantom of the darkness below me. Uncle Brook slowly raised his rifle, trying to get positioned without moving noticeably. He was just about in position to take the shot when, like a bolt of lightning, the phantom leaped into the darkness and totally disappeared from view! A split second later he would have been killed, but in that instant something frightened the leopard and he was gone, not to return again.

We all three sat there in disbelief and silence for some time. Then the tracker said that we might just as well go because he was sure the leopard would not return again that evening. We slowly climbed down from the *machung,* returned to the camp and spent the rest of the night there by the bank of the river.

The next morning the sun rose, and the beautiful jungle appeared out of the darkness. One of my most unforgettable memories ended with a love for the jungle and all it held in store for a young missionary's kid.

I have thought of this experience many times through my life and thought that even though we did everything right we did not accomplish the goal we set out to accomplish. That goal was to kill a leopard that had been a problem to that village.

In our lives we often see the same type of a situation; everything was done right—which included the planning and carrying out of a good plan—and it didn't work. The answer is to make sure that we do not quit doing the things we *should* do and it will work out some time in the future.

If we belong to the Lord Jesus we know that we often need to be reminded that He will strengthen us and cause us to have victory in His time and for His purpose. I think sometimes we feel that we have failed in something we have done when, in the end, it was a victory in making us persevere in our lives. The Bible says that in due time we will succeed if we do not faint. My thought for each is to "keep on keeping on and looking up."

The other thing I want to remind each one of us is that in the midst of all the dangers in life we are safe and protected. As I felt safe on that *machung* because Dr. Brock was there, so we too as we stay close to Jesus in

His safety *machung*, our salvation, we then can face the dangers of life and know that He is our protector on this life's journey. So be sure to trust Him and remember to keep looking unto Jesus who is the author and finisher or our faith.

CHAPTER 14

Raja, My Pet, and Me!

The cream of memories that I have from my boyhood is the memory of my pet royal Bengal tiger whose name was Raja, which means King. All of this took place when my father was on tour in the Dirang District of Assam. My father had been speaking and was stopping for lunch when some wood cutters came to him and handed him a baby tiger. They told him that the mother was killed and they wanted to give the *sahib* a gift for his son. I don't know how my father agreed to all of this, but when he came home there was the most beautiful little tiger kitten I had ever seen. My mother was not too thrilled with the idea of having a tiger running around the house, but she reluctantly agreed to it. My father then sat me down and told me that we would not be able to have Raja too long because he would get big very quickly and could not be kept around the house or the yard. He said that one day when Raja would get to be that big we would then have to send him to the zoo in Calcutta. I agreed to all he had said, but all I could think of was that I had a pet tiger, and that was incredible. My friends all came to see Raja, but they were not too thrilled to hold him even at that size. When he came to us his eyes were not open yet and he needed to be given milk every few hours. That turned out to be a problem for all. I was thrilled to feed him in the day time, but didn't do very well in the night time. I am sure that many times my father did some rethinking about bringing him to our home.

As the days went by Raja grew incredibly fast, in fact it seemed that he grew several inches every week. I would take him for walks and enjoyed seeing people moving away from me. Most of the people in our jungle area did not like tigers of any size because many had friends or family who had been killed by a tiger from the jungle.

Time went by and Raja grew and became a problem to feed. We mostly fed him chicken, and anything else that could be found. Raja was an unbelievable pet, but he was becoming a problem in many ways for all who had to help me take care of him.

One day I was playing with him in the yard when he knocked me down and grabbed me by the back of my neck and started to drag me around. He was playing with me, but his play was now the play that would equip him for life in the jungle. My father was walking from his office and saw this entire episode take place. He became concerned about my pet. He immediately came to me and said the time had come for Raja to go to the zoo in Calcutta. I tried to defend Raja but to no avail. The next morning a crate was made for him, and he was shipped by train to the zoo in Calcutta. This was a very sad day for me, but I knew in my heart that it was the right thing to do. He could not be turned out to the jungle again because the jungle tigers would kill him since he was not raised there. The only way to make sure he could live would be to send him to the zoo. I was lost without my Raja, and I did cry over my loss, but everybody in our household was thrilled not to have that great responsibility.

Time went by and finally the day came for me to go to a British boarding school at Woodstock in North India. The plans for my going were made and it was decided the two single missionaries and one missionary couple would escort six of us missionary kids to school. Our trip went through Calcutta where we waited for several days to get a train to Delhi and then on to Lucknow. We then went on by bus to the boarding school.

When we arrived in Calcutta the question was asked what we wanted to do. I immediately said I wanted to go to the zoo. I had already talked to the other kids and told them of my plan and why I wanted to go to the zoo. They all agreed! The ladies agreed with our thoughts, and the next day we went to the zoo.

When we got into the zoo I made a beeline for the tiger area. When I got there I looked at the tigers in every cage to see if I could see which one had Raja in it. I spotted one and thought it was Raja. I shouted out my greeting to him, and he jumped up and immediately he recognized me! The tiger keeper was standing close to me and asked if this was my tiger. I told him of Raja being my pet. He told me that he knew that it had to have been someone's pet tiger because he was so very tame. He told me that he took him for walks throughout the zoo, by placing a chain around his neck, and he even let people pet him. I asked if I could get close to the cage and he said, "Yes," and let me through the barrier up to the cage. I spoke to Raja and he lay down by the bars of the cage. I reached my hand in and stroked him under his neck. I cannot tell you the feelings I had as I stroked the *huge* tiger that once was my *little* tiger. As I talked with the man who took care of the tigers, I asked if there was any way that I could get in the cage with Raja. He told me to follow him. We came to the back of the cage and he unlocked the door and said to follow him and call Raja. I called Raja to me and he came over and lay down by my feet. He started to lick my leg and let me know that he was happy to be with me again. I was taken by the size of this tiger. He was huge—and here I was petting him!

As I was enjoying this moment, I looked out and saw my schoolmates coming, and the two lady missionaries accompanying them. When they saw me they all screamed with excitement, but one of the ladies looked at me, shrieked and fainted dead away! Things changed rapidly and people came to see what the problem was and tried to help the lady who had fainted.

Well, I will tell you that I had problems because of my actions, but I will not tell you the details at this writing. Suffice it to say, I was on restriction from that time on till we got to the boarding school and I was turned over to those who would have authority over me for the school year.

As a missionary kid I will have to say that this event has been relished in my memory all the years since that day. Often when I think of my pet tiger, and think of him as a little tiger kitten with his eyes not yet open and then petting the huge royal Bengal tiger in Calcutta Zoo, I am amazed at the experiences that I have had as a result of being a missionary's kid. It's astounding to think that none of this would have happened to me if my father and mother hadn't said that they would go to the farthest corner of the world to serve the Lord Jesus.

What an experience I had in life; when I think of it I am sure that it was certainly different. I have often thought of this time in my life and realized that this was a gift given to me. I have understood that I am rich in life experiences and lessons and that God has a requirement for my life as I have lived these many years. Remember that God isn't interested in giving you the worst, but the very best. May I suggest that each one of us trust Him and let Him give us that which will fulfill the purpose He has for our lives.

Often I think of the life I had as a missionary kid and recall the thoughts I have heard from many who say "Oh, you poor little person who has had to live in such conditions." Then I respond that I was never a poor little missionary kid, but one that has been given privileges and opportunities very few have been given. I grant you that it really was a difficult life in many ways, but when you have a mother and father like I had, who took time to make their jungle home a place of security, purpose and fun, I was the richer. As I have lived my life now I have tried to pass that kind of life and security onto my family.

When we are living to fulfill the purpose of the Lord with a right attitude, "life then is really worth living." So live for Him and enjoy the abundant life He has promised.

CHAPTER 15

Don't Be a Dumb Monkey!

One of the most memorable experiences I ever had took place in northern Ceylon (now Sri Lanka), many years ago. My wife, Shirley and I were missionaries there. Every once in a while when we would get a little break my wife would say, "You have been working hard; why don't you go out to the jungle and let the wind blow through your brain so you will be refreshed for the next school year." This I did—sometimes!

I asked my colleague, Bruce Ker, to go with me. He agreed and we packed our tent and hunting gear and set out for the northern part of the country where there were leopard, buffalo, elephant and, of course, crocodile. All of this made the jungle an interesting place, especially when all you have is a tent between you and the entire jungle world!

We took the car as far as we could and then hired a jeep to take us into the jungle. We were about 15 miles from the nearest village and set up our camp next to a little river. Today, with all the terrorist movements, this would not be possible, but at that time it was wonderful as we lived the jungle experience of a lifetime.

We shot a deer for food the first day and it was very good to have this fresh meat for our meals. Our cook took one of the hind quarters and buried it so that the heat would leave the meat, and later that night we had a jungle feast.

The interesting thing about me is that I love the jungle so much I just want to see God's real, authentic zoo and be a spectator in the midst.

The only time I kill an animal is for food or if it has killed somebody or is a rogue, destroying villages. I have loved the jungle since I was a very small boy.

One day I left camp very early in the morning and experienced one of the most interesting events in a jungle that has both leopards and monkeys among its residents. I was walking along listening to the noises of the jungle and loving every minute of my time there. All of a sudden I heard the shrieking of monkeys and the shaking of limbs of trees enough to get the attention of everything else around. I looked ahead of me and slightly up and I spotted the tree filled with monkeys. One time before I had experienced this in the jungles of North East India and knew I was in for a real jungle drama!

I noticed a tree that had fallen down between me and the tree full of monkeys. Immediately I got down on my hands and knees and approached the downed tree. As I moved along I looked up at the tree and saw the monkeys all staring down and screaming at something on the ground. When I got to the downed tree I carefully looked over the tree ahead to see what the monkeys were all looking and screaming at. What I saw was a beautiful, large leopard lying out in the open so all the monkeys could see him. He was a beautiful male that was doing something very clever to get the attention of what he thought could be his next meal.

His entire body was motionless except for his tail. It was slowly moving from side to side, and this motion was getting the attention of the monkeys. As I looked I saw that one monkey especially was seemingly mesmerized, moving his head from one side to the other watching the movement of the leopard's tail. All of a sudden the monkey shrieked and started to shake the branch he was on, vigorously scolding the leopard for what he was doing. Then the monkey came down one branch. Again the monkey started looking at the tail, moving his head from side to side as if in a trance. The leopard didn't move except for his tail that moved from side to side. The monkey again screamed at the leopard, shaking the branch he was on and scolding him madly. Then he came down one more branch, again intrigued by the movement of the tail. As I watched for a long time I realized that the monkey was so interested in the motion of the tail he didn't allow his natural fear of the leopard to control him. This repeated itself for almost a half hour. Then all of a sudden the monkey came down one more branch, and the leopard sprang up with a deafening roar to the branch and grabbed the curious monkey and ran off into the jungle to enjoy his dinner! All this because of a dumb monkey's inquisitiveness! To me that was one of the most interesting mornings I have ever spent in the jungle.

This is a picture of the problem with the temptations placed before us as people, especially young people. We are mesmerized by these temptations and slowly succumb to them; before long we are in the grasp of evil, and we cannot escape! I have often talked to young people and said as I recall this story, "Don't be a dumb monkey." The evil one wants to tempt each one of us to do evil and keep us from eternal life given to us by the Lord Jesus who can deliver each one of us from deceit and destruction.

I trust this story will cause you to make sure that you have a relationship with the Lord Jesus. That relationship comes from the moment we acknowledge we are sinners and the Lord Jesus is the Savior who can be *our* Savior when we ask Him to save us. After that we will not have to worry about acting like that dumb monkey who lost his life because he didn't pay attention to his inner senses. Don't act like this dumb monkey as you live your life. Pay attention to that which is right.

Remember, right choices in life will produce good memories later in life. Wrong choices will produce sorrowful memories in life. Today is the day when you will make some choice that you will live with tomorrow. His best is always reserved for those who *want* His best for life.

CHAPTER 16

The Man-Eating Leopard and the Villagers

One of my special friends in Ceylon (now Sri Lanka), was a man whose name was Hani Koch. He was one of the greatest hunters of the nation and was known by all who wanted to have an expert hunter with them when they went on their hunts. The thing he was known for the most was his concern for the common village people who had trouble with wild elephants and killer leopards. When a village would have trouble with an elephant becoming rogue or a leopard becoming a man eater they would get a message to him in Colombo, and he would go and help them out as soon as he could.

I had the privilege of meeting him one day when I needed to get my rifle registered at the local authorities. We introduced ourselves to each other; from that moment we began a friendship that lasted through the years of our being in Ceylon. I mentioned that I had grown up in India, and he said he had grown up in Ceylon. His parents were of Dutch extraction, having been in the country for several generations. Our families became fast friends and spent time together. When he found out that I had been on many hunts in India, he asked if I would like to go with him the next time he went. I, of course, said "Yes."

One day about four months later he came to see me telling of a village that had contacted him about a leopard that had killed nine people. They desperately wanted him to come and kill it. He asked if I would like to go along with him and take care of this problem. Thankfully, I found it *would* be possible and said I'd love to go with him.

Two days later our Jeep was packed, the permits were in hand, and we were on our way to a remote village in the northwest part of the country. We drove all day, coming to the village about dusk. When we got there the chief man of the village came to Hani and thanked him over and over again. By this time it seemed as if everybody in the village also came to welcome us. Hani was the main man, but it seemed they were very glad to see me too.

They served us tea and some local goodies that we ate sparingly. Afterwards we heard the stories of how several children had been snatched from the village by this leopard; others told of family members who had been out cutting wood and were attacked and killed. Honestly, after hearing all this we felt great anger against this jungle killer and knew that it had to be destroyed.

May I just say here that most of the jungle animals, including elephants, tigers and leopards, have an innate fear of man and will not seek to do harm unless there is some reason for that to have changed. This fear has been instilled by God, I am sure, because they are much stronger than man, yet they will leave man alone most all of the time. Their action now was maybe that they were getting too old to kill their natural prey or they had been injured in some way so they could not act naturally. Anyway, when this occurs they will have to be put down so the village can live in peace.

Hani Koch was their hero, their deliverer, and now had come to be their help again. I think that it is good for us to know that when we belong to the Lord Jesus and give Him our lives to gaurd and control, we then have a hero, a deliverer, and one who will protect us. I couldn't help but think of this as I observed the villagers and their adoration of Hani, my friend.

The head man sent two of the men from the village to show us where the last kill was, which thankfully, was a cow. We had walked for some time to find the kill, and now it was rather dark. Our tents were put up about a mile and a half from where the kill was, and we prepared for the night in the jungle. Sufficient wood was gathered so we would have a fire all night, and then a meal was prepared and we ate.

After dinner Hani and I took our guns and walked toward the carcass. We listened carefully to hear if there was any growling anywhere, but didn't hear or see anything. At the same time we both felt as though we were being followed by something. Since Hani was the more experienced hunter, I didn't think it was just *my* feeling. On several occasions we would stop as we thought we heard something, but then, nothing. This was repeated several times, but to no avail so we just walked back to camp rather confused. We went to bed for several hours and got up about three o'clock in the morning and returned carefully to the kill. We checked the direction of the wind so we would not arouse the suspicions of the leopard if he were around. As we walked back to the kill, we saw some leopard tracks that were on top of some of our tracks made as we returned to our camp last night. Hani looked at me and said that we indeed were being followed last night. Then he said that a leopard will often hunt those who are hunting him. Wow, what a realization! It was very obvious that we had a very cunning leopard now looking for us. We stayed there till about seven in the morning, but nothing showed itself so we returned to camp and had some tea and a good breakfast, after which we decided to lie down for a little rest.

Hani wanted to get several fresh kills around the area that day so that the leopard would have a chance to eat something fresh. The new kills were all in the general area of the old kill so the leopard would still be in that area.

We also had a *hide* built out of some bushes where we could sit and watch the kills without being noticed. The *hide* was made so that a tracker would be facing one way and each of us facing other directions so we could keep an eye on the kills and everything around.

After doing all of this we made sure we got some rest in the afternoon, even though it was so very hot and humid, but we knew that we needed some rest if we were going to be out for much of the evening.

About five in the afternoon we had some tea and a little refreshment and then went to the *hide* that we had prepared in the afternoon. As the afternoon melted into the evening, we felt a slight jungle breeze and we loved it when, all of a sudden, a wild elephant trumpeted near us and sent our hearts into triple beat! There was nothing more but the sound of the elephant moving off onto the jungle, and then silence again.

Hours went by as the jungle came to life with all the noises that let us know that there were many kinds of animals out there, but no leopard. About midnight Hani told the tracker and me that we might as well go back to camp because the leopard would not come now. We slowly returned to camp and had a cup of tea and went to our cots. The fire was going quite well so we felt good about our protection.

We both fell into an exhausted sleep and slept for several hours when, all of a sudden, we both woke up with a start and became conscious that we were being watched from the other side of a fire that had almost gone out! The light from the glowing embers was reflecting on two fiery, yellow eyes looking across our campsite right at us.

Very slowly each of us picked up our guns from the side of our cots and, without consulting with each other, fired in the direction of the eyes. Immediately the leopard sprang into the air and let out the most blood-curdling shriek I had ever heard and he fell down just in front of the fire! We both approached the leopard very cautiously, taking some sticks and throwing them at the leopard, but there was no movement. The leopard was dead. Wow, we looked at each other and hugged each other, very thankful that we had survived a cunning leopard that would have nothing to do with our prepared kills, but rather was stalking *us* and ready to make new kills of *us!* Upon examining the leopard we found that it had killed a porcupine, leaving some quills in his front paw which became infected. That is why he had become a man-eater and been a threat to the village. This was good for us to know so that we could tell the villagers why he had become a menace.

The other most memorable part of that evening was that Hani started asking about life and its meaning and destination. It was amazing to hear of his spiritual search and how his religious life was mostly for show before people. I was really surprised when he told me that he had been watching me for many months and had come to hear me speak. He said there was something about the messages I gave that had made him feel that what he had heard was real. He really wanted to know and then asked me to tell him again how he might be sure to go to heaven. He said, "Jim, we could have been killed, and I do not know where I would be if I would have died tonight." I grabbed my Bible and flashlight and showed him John 3:16:

> "For God so loved the world, that he gave his only begotten
> Son, that whosoever believeth in him should not perish, but
> have everlasting life."

Then I read Romans 3:23 about the fact we are all sinners:

> "For all have sinned and come short of the glory of God."

Then I read Romans 6:23, how the Lord Jesus gave the free gift of salvation to as many as called upon Him:

"For the wages of sin is death; but the gift of God is eternal
life through Jesus Christ our Lord."

Next, Romans 10:13:

"For whosoever shall call upon the name of the Lord shall be
saved."

After explaining all of this, Hani and I got on our knees and my
friend became a child of God by repenting and then calling upon the Lord
Jesus to be his Savior. May I say this was the greatest big-game trophy I
ever got from my time in the jungle!

By this time the village had heard the shooting and they came
running to where our camp was, shouting and yelling because they knew
that we had gotten the killer leopard. The trackers had lit the torches in our
camp, and the villagers saw the dead leopard on the ground. They came
over to us, putting their foreheads on our feet, a native way of honoring one
that they greatly admired and a way of expressing their thanks to us. They
brought their children in the middle of the night to thank us for making
their village safe once again. Their expression to Hani was as though
they were thanking a god. What a night to be there to see all of this and
hear the thoughts of their safety now. I was amazed by the expression of
appreciation from them and couldn't help thinking of the deliverance that
the Lord could give them spiritually. I was asking the Lord to give me the
chance to tell the people about eternal deliverance when Hani quieted the
crowd and said he had just found peace in his heart and wanted his friend
to tell them how they could have peace in *their* hearts. So this I did, and
many spoke to me about coming back and explaining things further. Three
months later an evangelist went to this village to give the message of Jesus
Christ and salvation to a people who were very receptive. For this I have
been eternally grateful.

By the way, the leopard only had one bullet hole in it, and when
Hani examined it he said, "Your position was perfect to deliver the kill shot
so the skin is yours." I am sure that it was the bullet of this great hunter,
Hani Koch, that *really* killed the leopard. This man was kind and gracious
at what he said. Maybe—just maybe—it *was* my shot, but we will never
know! If you ever come to my home I will take you into my office and
show you the skin of the leopard on my wall and remind you of the story

that said it had killed nine people.

As you live your life just remember the evil one is constantly stalking you and wanting to destroy your life. Be watchful and diligent to walk with the Lord Jesus and know that He is the one who said, "I will never leave you nor forsake you." Keep your heart fixed on His Word so that you will be spiritually strong and be able to live an abundant life.

Remember, live your life for Him and you will not have any regrets as you grow older.

CHAPTER 17

Intrigue with a Jungle Giant

During the years we lived in Ceylon (now Sri Lanka), many things happened. Many of them produced some great memories which we took away from our years in that land as a family, including times when we went on vacation to the hills of Ceylon. Jim and John learned the laws of the jungle and survival. I often had the privilege of going with them and tried to teach them the way to enjoy the jungle and, I might add, *that* they did.

One of them was when my wife Shirley's father came from the U.S.A. to live with us. Shirl's mother had passed away, and her dad was alone, so we invited him to come and live with us. Many things were so very different for him, coming from the city of Chicago. First of all he could not get over the many people everywhere, the heat and humidity of the country and the joy of really being with his daughter and his grandchildren. Honestly, he felt as though he was really living a dream, and he simply loved it.

He became the barber for our boys and me. Since he had four sons he knew how to do that, and do it well. He loved seeing and being with the boys. Our Jim being the oldest took it upon himself to make sure that all the neighbors met his grandfather. He tried to get him to ride our cook's bike, but was met with, "I would rather walk." He, having been a mail carrier in Chicago, also did that very well.

We went to Nuwara Eliya in the mountains of Ceylon for a vacation with him. We rented a little cabin with dirt floors and a thatch roof—and we spent fifty cents a day! What a wonderful time we had together for such a special price.   The boys were so excited about being in the cool and also being able to show their grandfather the mountain jungles.

Shirley's father was thrilled with this part of the country and loved to go exploring. One morning we all got up, and he was not there. We looked everywhere and were becoming very concerned. After several hours of looking frantically and asking the boys all about their grandfather, if they knew anything at all, Jim came up to us and said he did. He said that Grandpa had told him he was going for a walk across the valley and up the mountain on the other side. He said that if he didn't get back that he should tell Dad and Mom where he was. We all left the house and started walking down the path through the valley, when we all spotted him coming up the path! He said he was sorry to be late, but you could see that he had had a great experience even though he was a little late. He was a great walker so he had no problem walking, but I said he should never do that again in case he *did* have a problem and we would not know where he was.

Jim was very happy that he had been the one with the special knowledge about his grandfather. It was wonderful how much the boys loved having him there.

One of the things he really wanted to do was to experience seeing a real live elephant in the jungle. This was one thing that had intrigued him when he found out that he would be coming to Ceylon with its jungles.

One day my special friend, Jerry Wanagasekera, mentioned that he would like to have us go on a hunt with him to the northeastern part of the country. I thought that would be a great thing so I contacted my missionary colleague, Bruce Ker, to see if he would like to go. His response was an immediate "Yes!" I then told Dad, and he was excited about the opportunity to go with us. It thrilled him to think he really would be able to see a jungle that was different from the "jungles of Chicago." That was exactly what I wanted for him.

We prepared the tents, planned for the food, checked the guns and, most of all, made sure that we knew exactly where we were going. My Shirl and the boys said goodbye to us, and we left for an adventure that we have not forgotten to this day.

Our trip took us to the northeastern part of the country on the main road. After many hours we arrived at a little village where Jerry made arrangements to hire a tractor with a trailer to take us many miles into the deepest jungle. I really thought we should have a Jeep, to make it more authentic as a hunt, but that was not available. It was *only* a tractor, but it beat walking those many hot, muggy miles! I will never forget how hot it was, and that we were following a trail more than a road. Dad thought it was very rough and shouldn't pass for a road—and we all agreed. Jerry knew exactly where we should go, as he was a national from Ceylon. I was excited for Dad because he would have the opportunity to see some wild elephants that he so wanted to see. This jungle was filled with many types of animals anyone would want to see: buffalo, leopard, crocodile, deer and many others.

As we were going along the trail in the heat and humidity we came to a river and I said, "Let's stop and take a dip in the cooling water." We simply went into the water with our clothes on and just let the cool water give us a new perspective on life. Our time in the water came to an abrupt end when one of the trackers told me that there were crocodiles in that river! All of us came out of the water quickly and returned to our trip into the deepest part of the jungle.

We kept going in the hot sun until late afternoon when we arrived at a beautiful camping spot in a small meadow. Close by there was a spring spilling over the rocks into a clear pool below. What an idyllic spot this was. Dad couldn't believe we would be spending the next number of nights here, but he was thrilled, to say the least.

The tents were put up and a fire pit was prepared. Then we all went looking for enough wood to keep a fire going through the night. Our cook, Thomas, asked us to shoot a deer for our supper that he would prepare. With all the many deer in the area it didn't take Jerry long to bring one in, cleaned and dressed, for Thomas. He took one of the rear legs and buried it to cool it so it would be better for what he had in mind for later in the evening. This was done to take the wild game taste and the heat out of the meat.

The two trackers made a three-cornered lean-to that faced the fire and prepared their bedding rolls for the night. Our tents were now up and prepared with our cots, and things were ready for the days ahead.

My friend Jerry, Bruce, Dad, one tracker and I went for a short hunt just to see what was in the area. We did not stay long, because it was getting toward evening, and we wanted to have a very special first evening together. Hunting is more about being together and experiencing the jungle than killing anything. It is amazing how your heart is so open, and the Lord has a chance to speak to you out in His great out-of-doors.

When we returned to camp our cook, Thomas, had a tremendous meal prepared from the venison we gave him, along with rice and curry. The moon was starting to come up over the jungle, and the trumpeting of elephants caused Dad to say that he might really get a chance to see an elephant so that his dream would come true. It was all so real, only to be made more special by sitting around the roaring fire and drinking tea. The evening breeze put a chill in the air and it was comfortable and very interesting as we heard the sounds of the jungle night surround us. Dad became a little concerned and asked if we were all right, and I said, "As long as we keep the fire going all will be well." All of us kept quite close to the fire as we told stories of our times in the jungles of that part of the world.

About ten o'clock in the evening we readied ourselves for bed, making sure that there was enough wood for the fire to last through the night. The watches were set so each one knew what hours through the night we were responsible for the fire. We went to bed, but sleep didn't come quickly to any of us because of the wild animals that seemed to want to explore what all this was that had not been here before. I had my gun ready by my side through the night. When it was my turn to watch the fire and the camp, Dad came out and said he couldn't sleep, so he would like to be with me if that was all right. This was a very special time, and we had the opportunity of talking of life and enjoying each other's company. I would like to say that he and I developed a tremendous relationship that created a family bond that lasted all the rest of his life.

Finally we all got a few hours of sleep and awakened early to go out on our early morning hunt. We had very early morning tea and then left to go into the jungle, following animal paths. Some people say that we who hunt just go out to shoot anything, but this is not this jungle man's thoughts. Rather, we go into the jungle to see the beauty and the wild life that can be seen and to learn from the animals and the jungle life. I have taught our sons that God owns the animals of the jungle and doesn't mind giving us one to eat, but not just to kill. Our motto is to kill only what you eat, and enjoy God's jungle in every other way. I might say that the jungle or forest is a good place to get to know who you really are and why you are here on earth. It is a good place to let some thoughts from the Bible get a deep set into your being. It will teach you how cunning animals have to live to survive and live in a place where they have to always be on their keenest alert. This ought to teach *us* how to live in a world that wants to destroy our Christian faith.

After hunting and observing all morning we returned to camp and ate lunch; then we took a little nap, had a cup of tea and left for the afternoon hunt. Jerry and Bruce took one of the trackers and went in one direction and Dad, the other tracker and I went another way and said we would meet back at camp in the early evening.

We had been walking and observing for several hours when we decided to sit down and have a little refreshment. As we were sitting there we heard a crackling in the jungle as if someone was breaking a branch off of a tree. My tracker quietly said that there was a big elephant about 50 yards to our right. We determined to see if the wind was blowing in the right direction to hide our scent. It was, so we slowly walked toward the direction we knew the elephant was going. I wanted Dad to see the elephant in the wild, but I was a little concerned as we followed our tracker. As we moved along we saw that the jungle was thinning and an opening was just in front of us. We stopped and looked—and all of a sudden this elephant came out into the opening! I couldn't believe my eyes because it was the biggest wild elephant I had ever seen, and I have seen *quite* a few. It was old because the hair on its back was reddish. It was really the jungle giant of Dad's dreams. I was so taken by the sight I didn't notice that Dad had stepped out into the opening and was taking a few steps toward the elephant—so he could get a better look, I guess. My heart almost stopped as this jungle giant looked his way and kept going. I quickly stepped out and took Dad by the shoulders and carefully pulled him back into the covering of the jungle. The tracker kept looking at the elephant and motioned that we should move back farther into the jungle. As we did, the elephant turned in our direction for a few steps, and then kept moving on his way.

I will tell you that I breathed a sigh of relief and thanked the Lord for His protection. There is no doubt that God gave this present to Dad as his gift from the jungle. We made our way back to camp because it was getting toward evening and because we were hot and hungry and wanted to get back to the safety of the camp.

When we arrived, Thomas greeted us with a cup of tea and became the first one to hear Dad's tale of the incredible elephant he had seen. As the others came into camp the tale was told again.

Before we sat around the campfire to eat that night we all went into the spring-fed opening in the ground and enjoyed a refreshing bath and relief from the heat and sweat of the day. Then we sat down to eat and enjoy the jungle night as it settled in on all of us. It must have been about midnight when we heard a tremendous trumpeting by an elephant and it got our attention immediately! We waited and waited to see if we would have company in our camp, but nothing ever came. Maybe it is because the trackers built the fire to a tremendous blaze! I think the elephant Dad had seen had to come by to say it was good to see you, "King Gustav." Dad was from Sweden, and his name was Gust, and I would often speak of him being the king in our family.

We stayed there for a few more days, but the event of the hunt was about Dad and his real, live elephant from the jungles of Ceylon. When he got home he had to tell his daughter and his grandchildren of the great adventure in the jungle.

As I have thought of this experience in the years that followed I have come away with the joy of family relationships. How very rich they can be when we take time to be with each other. Shirley's dad lived with us for more than six months, and he said that his time with us was the most wonderful time he had ever had with his daughter since she grew up, because of the length of time he spent with us. Our family was enriched by his being with us and this experience was one that thrilled Dad.

When a family is involved together and they belong to the Lord Jesus there is a joy and an enrichment that others do not have. Shirley's dad knew the Lord as his Savior and his life enriched all of us, which included his grandsons. I would say take time to be together and allow time for each other and all will be enriched.

The Bible says in John 10:10b: "I am come that you might have life and that you might have it more abundantly." Expect it and live it.

Your life will not have this type of adventure, most likely, but fathers, take your family out and away from the daily routine and just be together, and you will find that the memories you make will be remembered in the days that are ahead. Be sure to do something now because you won't have the privilege of doing these special things for long.

We can't do that with Dad any more because we are not together any more, and memories cannot be made again here on earth. We are thankful, though, that Dad is with his Lord whom he loved while here on earth with us.

Please take every opportunity and invest your time together because it won't last too long. This is my injunction to you!

CHAPTER 18

The Jungle Gaur and a Tiger Encounter

When I drive into our garage, facing me is one the most interesting trophies in the world. It is a world-record trophy from the jungles of South India, a jungle ox, a gaur. Whenever I see it my thoughts go back to a night in 1962 when I almost lost my life to a tiger. What a story!

In 1962 we were living in the island nation called Ceylon (now Sri Lanka), just off the southern coast of India. For some time we had desired to go to South India for a vacation. We got all the necessary paper work done and then made arrangements to take the night train from Colombo to Jaffna, the northern most city in the country. The train ride was great fun and our boys, Jim and John, just loved it, as did we. This trip was one of the most memory-making trips of our lives. Sleeping on the bunks and rocking back and forth was neat, and we really enjoyed it. The next morning we got on a ship that went from Jaffna to Dhaniskoti, the southern most city in India. The ship trip was very special as we went toward India, my country. On the ship we had breakfast consisting of fried eggs over rice and then, of course, tea. I don't think Jim and John enjoyed the eggs too much, but it was filling and safe. The boys always wanted to listen to me tell them about my country and all its jungles and tigers, and now they were going to the country I had talked about so often. We got off the ship and transferred to a train to go to our destination in the mountains of south India.

Before we could get on the train we had to walk about a mile in the hot sun and sand to the government office to get our passports stamped and get permits to stay in India for a month. The boys couldn't understand why the office was not at the station instead of being a mile away across the hot, dusty plains. It was so hot that our John got overheated as a result of being out in the sun. As we got back to the train station we immediately went to the pump in the middle of the platform and had John stand under it as I pumped water all over him. Then we got some cucumbers and peeled them and had him eat them. They are one of the only things available that one can eat to cool the body off from the inside. It was interesting that Jim was very hot but didn't seem to be bothered very much. Thankfully it worked, and both boys did well the rest of the trip.

The train left the station and we traveled for the rest of the day and came to the city where we were met by one of the Christian leaders who took us to his house where we stayed the night. I don't think we have ever been so hot! Even Jim had a lot of trouble with that night, so we had to come up with an idea to help us through those hours. When we went to bed we sprayed our sheets with water and let the little breeze bring us some natural air conditioning. We managed by sleeping out on the roof of the house for a portion of the night. The next morning our friends met us in a Jeep station wagon, and we started up the hills to Kodaikanal where the missionary children's school was located.

The trip up the hill was incredible as the climate got cooler with every thousand feet of altitude we rode. Jim even commented that all of us seemed to change for the better the higher we got in altitude. By the time we reached 7,000 feet we were actually cool and needed a sweater!

Our time was unbelievable as we all recuperated from our hot weather in Colombo and felt like we were getting healthy again. Nobody really knows how run down one gets in the hot, humid tropics. The mountains really cool you off and you feel like living again!

When we finally got to the hill station we were greeted by the missionary kids and welcomed into the place we were going to stay for the month of vacation. Jim and John were thrilled to meet so many new friends. The boys were put into the boys' dorm section with the younger missionary kids who were there for school. It was amazing how they fit into the schedule of the school dorm and loved it. They did not miss us it seemed, and we were thrilled that they fit in so well. Shirl and I were taken into a nice little room with a tin roof, and we loved it, especially when it rained. Here we were all feeling like a million dollars being out of the tropics. Jim and John both came to us, asking why we couldn't do the Lord's work in a climate like this. We both concurred with their feeling, because our favorite place is in the mountains in the tropics.

One of the things that my friend wanted me to do with him was to go hunting—and that we did. Mostly we just walked up and down the mountains and took in the sights of the magnificent jungle.

While we were there one of the *maharajas* (king) came to the area and killed a magnificent tiger. I went to see it after it had been killed, and I was really sick to see this beautiful jungle king killed just for sport. The tiger was not a man-eater nor had he harmed anyone in the villages, but some king wanted him as a trophy. This is why tigers in India are a vanishing species, and it is such a pity.

One of the animals they wanted was a jungle ox called a *gaur.* They are immense and not afraid of tigers or anything else in the jungle, except an elephant. The thought was that maybe we could get one of them and then give the food to the non-Hindus in the villages around the area, and thus make it possible for some of the Christians to have contact with them.

My friend, Vern, and I made plans to go into an area and see if it were possible to get one. The people of the village said that there were some nearby. One of our trackers and I started out on a motorcycle ahead of Vern, who was going to come as soon as he could. We made arrangements ahead of time where we would meet in the jungle area and at what time. Then the tracker and I left. We traveled down the *ghat road* for about seven miles and then went down a jungle path for about seven or eight miles. The path was very steep, and finally I said to the tracker, who was riding behind me, that I was afraid I would not be able to get the motorcycle out of the area later because it was so very steep. We came to a woodcutter's house and made arrangements to leave the motorcycle with him.

My tracker wanted to know if I knew how to track in the jungle and I said "Yes." He was very happy and we went on into the mountains looking for any sign of a jungle *gaur.* After we had been tracking for a long time we came on to some *gaur* tracks and spotted some tracks that were very large. These tracks went off alone up a valley between the mountains. As we kept following them we spotted him. He was huge! We went up on one side of the valley and when we were able to get the right angle for a shot at the *gaur* in the valley below us, I took aim and shot him. He turned to come toward us and I shot again and he went down. We realized we had a trophy to be sure. We also were sure he would feed many of the people in the villages because they were not Hindus.

I made arrangements with the tracker to make sure the people of the village would get the meat. Then I started thinking about my friend and that it was about time to meet him. May I say again that God owns the animals in the jungles and will give you one if needed, but never just waste the gift He gives. We made sure it wasn't wasted. This was not the story, however!

I told my tracker that I needed to go and meet my friend. He looked at me and said, "Sir, there are tigers here, and I have no gun. I would be much safer if I had a gun." Then is when I made my *first* mistake and left my gun with him! I told him that later in the evening the village people would be down to divide the meat because they had heard the sound of the gun and knew there would be food for the feast the next day. I also instructed him what to do with the head and horns if I didn't return. At this point I was planning on returning to him with my friend.

It was starting to get quite dark by the time I reached the place where I was to meet my friend, but he was not there. I was becoming quite concerned, to say the least, because I thought that my friend had gotten in trouble. In the jungle when you say that you will be somewhere it is a rule that you *are* there. If not, then you know there is a problem. I was not sure what to do, but I thought I needed to go back up the path to see if my friend had gotten in trouble along the way.

I ran up the path and got to the woodcutter's house and asked him about my friend. He said that he did not know anything about him; that made me even more concerned. I gave him a little money for keeping the motorcycle and rode it toward the highway. It was getting quite cold and then it started to rain and soaked my motorcycle so it finally stopped. I was very concerned about the motorcycle because it belonged to another person. Because of the ban on imports these bikes were very valuable, so I just kept pushing. After some time I started to feel sick and I realized that I was getting altitude sickness because of the difference in altitude from where I lived in Colombo, which was at sea level. This elevation was about 6,000 feet.

I finally sat down, so very sick and very upset with myself for having gotten into this mess. But the worst was yet to come! As I was sitting there I heard the voice of a man singing in the jungle, making sure he was making enough noise to let the tigers and other animals know that he was coming through. I shouted to him and really scared him, but he came to me and I told him that I needed help to get the motorcycle out of this place. I asked if he could go up to the village and get several men to come down to help me. He told me that he would be glad to help but that he could go much faster if he had a flashlight! That is when I made my *second* mistake as I gave him my flashlight. He was gone and I was relieved, but while I was thinking about all of this the roar of a tiger came echoing through the valley on my right. The sound was blood chilling; the hair on the back of my neck seemed to rise, and my heart started to pound. To be honest, I had been close to tigers much of my life and I didn't feel this would be a threat, but have you ever had a tiger roar as you were alone in the jungle's darkness? Let me inform you that there is no more intimidating sound than a roaring tiger in the jungle when you are all alone.

Some time went by when another roar from the tiger echoed up the valley, only now it was much closer. I knew that tigers won't bother you unless they are threatened or they are man eaters. I had not heard anyone talking of anything like that since I had come to the mountains, but here I was alone with this animal—and I felt very alone! I did move up the path a little distance, but I became so very ill I thought I couldn't go on—so I stopped, becoming sicker and sicker. If you ever have had a bad case of altitude sickness then you know that you are sure that death isn't far away! I tried to be quiet so the tiger would not know where I was, but he had heard me, I am sure, because in a few minutes there was a tremendous roar, and the distance from me was much closer.

I prayed and told the Lord what a stupid thing I had done, and I began to realize that I could be in big trouble. I was feeling very sick and awfully wet and cold. The temperature was down in the forties and I was shivering very hard. I had a picture appear in my mind of our mission paper with the headlines, "MISSIONARY KILLED BY A TIGER." Then the picture in my mind was of two little, old ladies saying to each other, "If he had been doing missionary work he would not have been killed!"

All of a sudden there was a roar just in front of me, and I could smell the breath of the tiger, and it was really awful. I slowly got down into a ditch and dragged the motorcycle so I could pull it over me if the tiger decided to attack me. I am not sure if that would do any good, but it became my survival plan. It seemed like an eternity went by and no noise, then I heard the tiger move off to my right, and I thought I was out of danger. By the way, I didn't feel sick at all at that moment! The tiger walked some distance away, growling a little at a time and I really wondered what that was all about. Then, all of a sudden, the tiger turned around and came back, growling all the time. By this time I was really becoming concerned, especially when the tiger lay down across from me!

Just about that time I heard the men coming from the village and I slowly got up, but felt awful. On the other hand, I was greatly relieved. When the men came they didn't know the tiger was there and they started to argue about who would take the front end and who would take the back end of the motorcycle. All of a sudden the tiger gave a growl and the men and motorcycle moved up the path rapidly!

When we got to the road they helped me get the motorcycle started, I gave them some money and went to the bungalow where we were staying. When my Shirley saw me, she became very scared about how I looked. I was very strange looking from cold exposure and fatigue. She helped me into the shower to warm up, and I'm sure I drained all of the hot water out of the water heater. I stayed there for a long time! Finally, after I thawed out a bit we spoke to each other and we prayed because it was one of the most frightening experiences I had ever had in my life. There is more to the story, but I will leave it here because the Lord delivered me—and that was enough.

Many times I have thought of this incident and realized how close to being killed I really was. I thought of my own responsibility in this saga and what part of all of it was really my fault. Even though the idea of helping in the villages was a good one, some of the other things that I did were not the wisest. It came to me that the Lord often takes care of us even when we have made choices which could have been wiser ones. He has a plan for our lives and a purpose for our living. He cares for us even when we make decisions that could have been better ones, because He knows His full plan for our lives. Therefore He takes us through so our lives might be used by Him in the years ahead that are in part of His plan.

Remember, the Lord has a special plan for you, so live to accomplish the purpose He has for you in the life He has given you. Live life to the fullest because the Lord Jesus has the best for you. You know that you will have the best life when you have given the choice in living it to Him.

I don't think that I have ever lived through an experience in my life quite like this one. The intent was adventure but with a desire to do something good for many people. I have wondered if I was more interested in the adventure than helping three villages. When I get to heaven I'm sure the Lord will let me know!

It is a reminder to me that we don't have to be perfect for the Lord to protect us and use us. Just remember that we are His, and He doesn't stop protecting us sometimes when we do not make the best decisions in our lives.

Too soon our time in that beautiful place came to an end, and as we prepared to leave, Shirl and I were confronted by two young boys who had it all worked out with their new friends so that they could stay and go to school with them! It was hard to have to say, "No, we must leave and, yes, go back to the hot, humid place called Colombo!" That was the place where God had His special plan for us.

CHAPTER 19

Rescued by the Elephant Ropes!

In 1975, long after leaving India, while we were ministering in Hawaii, I received an invitation to come and speak at a conference for the churches of North East India. It was something I had wanted to do for many years. The invitation to go back to the place where I had been raised was a thrill to me. It was hard to get a permit to go into the area, but one of my boyhood friends was now a government official for this area so he made it possible for me to get the permit.

My Indian brother, Dr. Ben Wati, was behind the invitation to come to India and had made all the other arrangements for our getting into the area. My associate in the ministry in Hawaii, Paul Schultz, accompanied me on this trip. We arrived in Calcutta on the beautiful Pan Am Boeing 747 airplane, and then a few days later we boarded a DC-3, left over from World War II! Paul was quite shocked, especially when he saw some patched holes in the body of the plane! These were holes left over from being shot during the war.

It was quite an experience as we flew over my home country. I recognized many of the mountain villages where I had been as a boy. Memories were going crazy in my mind. Then we landed in Jorhat and proceeded to the mission compound where we were met by many, even some who had grown up with me there. What a time this was for me! This reminded me that we need to be sure we live life when we are young so we can have good memories when we get older.

We went by bus to the capital of Nagaland, Kohima, where the meetings were to be held. It was a joy to be able to minister to the representatives of thousands of churches. This is not the story, but I had to give a little background.

After the meetings Ben, Paul and I went to a special game reserve called Kaziranga National Park where there are many wild animals, including elephants, tigers and especially the Indian one-horned rhino. We arrived at a guest house where we stayed that night. We had hired an elephant to go into the jungle the next day, which caused each one of us to be quite excited. I had not been on an elephant in the jungle since I was a boy, so you can imagine how much I was looking forward to that day.

That evening we had a good dinner of rice and curry, which I relished in a special way, since *that* was what I ate often when I was a child. Sleep was slow in coming because of the jungle animals letting us know they were there.

The next morning we paid the fee to enter the park and proceeded to find our elephant, and all three of us climbed up on this huge animal of jungle transportation and settled on his back. There was a netting of ropes that went around the body of the elephant. When we were all on, the *mahout* instructed us about what we needed to do to be safe on the back of the elephant.

As we started through the jungle we saw many animals: wild elephants, deer of many kinds found only in India and wild boar. It was very exciting, and many pictures were taken of the animals—and each other too.

About noon we came to a special tree that had a platform in it and got off to have lunch and rest a little bit. The *mahout* said that we would be going into an area where there were tigers, and he told us that we should be sure to hold on to the ropes if the elephant saw a tiger. He said that if a tiger was spotted, the elephant could move very quickly to protect himself, and we could be thrown off if we did not hold on tightly to the ropes. At the time we did not realize how important this instruction would be for us in the next number of hours.

It was getting late into the afternoon, and we were going through a grassy area when, all of a sudden, the *mahout* stopped the elephant and pointed to his right. What a sight it was as we looked down to that area and saw the most beautiful royal Bengal tiger who was looking right up at us from where he was lying! This made the blood rush around in our bodies, I assure you, and our hearts pounded heavily. The elephant rumbled deeply from within, letting the tiger know that he was not afraid of him. We watched for about 30 or 40 seconds when, all of a sudden, the tiger got up and disappeared into the jungle. Wow, what a moment that was for us, a memory that has never left us.

We moved on, looking for a rhino because we had not seen one yet. Our *mahout* wanted to make sure that I would see one, as this was a return to *my* country. This I appreciated very much and was quite excited to see one.

As we were moving through the tall grass there was a movement that caught our attention. There before our eyes, coming out of the tall grass, stood a gigantic bull rhino that didn't seem too happy we were there. It seemed forever that we were looking at each other. The elephant was getting nervous as the rhino snorted at us, then made a charge toward us only to stop short. The elephant braced, but did not back away. This was going to be a jungle standoff, and we happened to be on the back of the object of his charge.

The *mahout* spoke reassuringly to the elephant and then said to *us* that we had better be ready because he thought the rhino was not going to go away. My brother Ben started praying out loud. Paul and I were praying silently when, all of a sudden, the rhino charged the elephant! There were some very quick movements by the elephant as the rhino came charging at us full speed. The elephant stood his ground and, as the rhino was about to pierce him with his horn, the elephant hit him with his trunk, spinning the rhino around and almost throwing us off the elephant! The ropes were our salvation as we hung on for dear life. The elephant again positioned himself to thwart another charge by the rhino. The moment was one being indelibly imprinted on our minds in slow motion it seemed.

The rhino charged again. The elephant hit him a tremendous blow with his trunk and knocked him to his knees. When the rhino got up he looked at the huge elephant and decided that he was bigger and stronger so turned and ran off into the jungle.

What a moment it was for us as we trembled along with the elephant, realizing we could have been in a lot of trouble if we had been knocked off the elephant. If it had not been for the ropes across the elephant's back we surely would have fallen off, and the results would have been quite different.

On the way back the *mahout* told us that this elephant had been charged and received quite a gash just three weeks before. The elephant had decided not to let that happen to him again, I guess; therefore his stand against the rhino said he would not run, but would fight. When we all returned from this adventure we were grateful for the deliverance for each of us by the Lord Jesus. The memories that we all took home with us might have been quite different.

This reminded me that in life we often go through some very difficult times and often dangerous times that can affect our character and our moral values in many ways. The interesting thing is that the Lord Jesus has promised that He would never leave us nor forsake us. In life He has given us ropes of deliverance that we must hold on to; then we will be able to survive what life throws at us. It is absolutely necessary to know the Lord Jesus as Savior and then walk with the Word of God as the guide and protection for life. I trust this experience will help you with a few lessons for your very special life.

In your life you more than likely will not be on the back of an elephant and be charged by a wild rhino in the jungle, but your life will be challenged by many things that the evil one will throw in your pathway. You will be attacked by evil in a way no jungle can match, but there is strength in the Lord Jesus. Your greatest challenge in your life might come from your peers and the pressure will be hard to resist. It is at a time like this that you need to look up to the Lord Jesus and ask for strength for that moment. *That* is the time to resist the pressure to sin and remember the Bible says, "Resist the devil and he will flee from you." Look around and see the results in those who didn't do that and are paying the price for their having given in to what was wrong.

Remember the statement of the apostle Paul, "I can do all things through Christ which strengthens me." Now go and live in the abundant life the Lord Jesus has promised.

CHAPTER 20

A Jungle Excursion and a Charging Rhino!

After many decades, in 1997, I had the privilege, with our son John, to return to North East India, the area where I grew up. We had been asked to speak to the leadership of the church in that part of India. We had been ministering for 3½ weeks and had spoken to the representatives of more than 7,000 churches. This was a joy that overwhelmed my heart because when I was a boy in that area there were human heads hanging on the walls of many houses. The British had put an end to the practice, but it was the left over from head-hunting days in that part of North East India. It was only when Christianity came into the area that head hunting actually stopped.

Our son John said he wanted to go back with me to the area close to where I lived in our first jungle home in North Lakhimpur. We decided that we would go to a special game reserve called Kaziranga to try to see some tigers and other game in the reserve.

We boarded an old bus and started out from Guwahati to Kaziranga for this special time together in my India. What a ride it was as we bumped along the road—and then broke a rim on one of the back wheels. We thought we were through with this bus, but finally the bus driver decided we could ride on the wheel even though it was badly broken. We proceeded with all the noise of a wheel that really wasn't working very well. The bus stopped at the next village, and we were transferred to another bus and were on our way again. That bus was not much, but we finally arrived at the reserve where we were to spend the night. The place where we stayed was on the edge of the jungle, but it was not out of range for tigers. John and I decided we would walk several miles to a place they said had a telephone so we could call his Dee and my Shirl. Just when we were going to start out a gaurd called out to us to tell us that it was too dangerous to walk because of the ever-present tigers at night. Needless to say we didn't go to make the call, especially after we had been told a tiger had killed a wild pig several feet from where we were going to stay.

That evening we had a good dinner in this special bungalow that the British had built during their day. It was good to be able to speak in my baby tongue to these people. To say the least, the place was rather old, but was great for memories from my childhood.

Later that evening a man came by to see us and to welcome us. There had been no information sent ahead, but the jungle telegraph had given the news to the people of the jungle area that the son and grandson of the missionaries who had worked here had returned.

He called me by name and welcomed me back into my home area and thanked me for bringing my son. Then he told us that he was a Christian and wanted to thank our family for bringing the message of the Lord Jesus to this area so many years ago. It really touched our hearts as we realized it was my folks who, along with their colleagues, were responsible for bringing the message of salvation to this people so many years ago. It was obvious that God's Word does not return without results.

We slept well that night and rose to a good breakfast. We were welcomed by a gaurd, who told us that he, too, was a Christian, so this is how our day started. The night before we had hired a Jeep to take us into the jungle, and so our safari started as we went deeply into this wild jungle area.

It wasn't long before we saw a big tusker elephant coming out of the jungle. At first we didn't see the *mahout* on his back, but as the elephant came out of the jungle we saw the man riding and controlling him. We stopped the Jeep to see this magnificent elephant and talk to the *mahout*. Our gaurd, Nyack, told us that this man is a Christian, too. His testimony was similar to the others we had met. All of this pointed back to the missionary work of my parents and their colleagues from the beginning days of missions in the area.

It was amazing to learn that the one that started the work in that jungle area was one of my father's students in his Bible training school whom I knew when I was a boy. I asked how many were in his jungle church and he answered "Three thousand four hundred." I was shocked and I asked him again in his language, which was my baby tongue, thinking he meant three hundred and forty. He looked at me and said, "Don't you think I know how to speak my own language?" I was a little shocked, but thrilled that the first figure was the right one! Again, what a thrill it was to know that the work of your parents and their colleagues had really been a remarkable success for the Lord. When this was learned, our son John said that he had never felt so attached to his roots as he did right then, even though he had never been in this area before.

The *mahout* offered to give our son a ride on the elephant, which he did *not* turn down. Already it had been a great day in the jungle. We continued into the jungle and saw wild boar, sambar, deer and a baby leopard running into the jungle to its mother. The trail took us over a very rickety bridge that made us a little nervous, but we made it! One of the things we came upon was a building that the gaurds used for their living quarters as they were on duty. The amazing thing was that this house was just like my home of years gone by in every detail. The statement our son made to me was that this was the end of the world and then 50 miles and was simply unbelievable that *his grandmother* had come to live here so many years ago!

As we continued into the jungle we came to a lake where we saw a herd of about 20 elephants as they played and ate grass from the bottom of the water. It was astounding to see them take a tuft of grass in their trunks and wash the mud off of the roots and then eat it!

As we were watching, all of a sudden we realized that there were elephants all around us! They started to trumpet and we became a little concerned because these elephants had now blocked our way out of the area. John stood up in the Jeep and took pictures and recorded everything. I will have to admit he was less concerned than I was. Very soon after that they started to leave. It was quite a relief to now be able to leave as well.

Our tracker wanted to have us see some Indian rhinos so we proceeded to another area through elephant grass which stands eight to twelve feet tall. Again we came to some water and grass along its banks. Our tracker thought it would be all right if we got out of the Jeep and walked around a bit. It did feel good to stretch and walk. As we were walking we saw the grass move and we knew there was a rhino moving through the area. We got down and waited when all of a sudden a beautiful rhino ran out of the tall grass into the open and stopped. The tracker told us not to move because the rhino does not have very good eyesight. That is *exactly* what we did! The rhino was trying to make out exactly what we were when all of a sudden he started to charge toward us. The tracker took the safety off on his gun and the click startled the rhino and it stopped in its tracks! We sat motionless for some time looking at this magnificent animal as he looked at us. I prayed to be sure, and asked the Lord again for His protection—and at that moment the rhino turned and ran back into the elephant grass and was gone. Our son, who is a very adventurous type, was thrilled beyond words—and his father was thrilled too.

We decided to go back slowly to see what else we could see, but the time for leaving the jungle was getting close. We proceeded to the entrance of the preserve, realizing that not every day does one get charged by a rhino when he decides to stop the charge and let you live another day!

What a memorable time we had during our visit to Kaziranga, and I will never forget our time together and the opportunity that I had with our son and, I trust, he with me. Again I must say it was a thrill returning to the area where I was raised and see the results of the work of the pioneer missionaries. It was unbelievable to see the thousands of Christians now in the area. I will have to say it was really thrilling to realize anew that God's Word *doesn't* return void.

I would like to say that as I thought of this experience in the many years that have gone by, it is rich in memory. To have had the opportunity to spend it with our son was a real thrill, but to have had the privilege of ministry together made it a tremendous blessing.

Often we hear people say that life as a Christian is very ordinary and boring, but I am here to say it is just the opposite. When you are living for the Lord in your life, know that when you give the choice in life to Him, He will give you the very best. So why not trust Him and live for Him?

If we have accepted the Lord Jesus as Savior we often seem to just live and nothing great seems to come our way. I would like to say that when I was a little boy I was not very concerned with what my parents were doing in their ministry work, but now it is a different story. I am much older now and have the privilege of looking back and realizing that the Lord will accomplish His plan through those who have given their lives to His service. It was not so important to me then, but now it is one of the greatest missionary stories of modern days. One of the greatest movements in missionary history took place in that area of the world.

This experience has made me more conscious of being what the Lord has planned for me to be and doing what He has designed for me to do in my life in accordance with His will.

Remember you are a part of God's plan for this time in history, so be sure you live with His plan in mind.

CHAPTER 21

Head Hunters Turned to Heart Hunters

These stories mostly took place in North East India. The reason I was there was because I had a mother and father who had given their lives to take the message of love, forgiveness, assurance and heaven to a people who had never known about the forgiveness of a loving God. Their only thought was to try to appease an angry god who was always trying to harm them.

In most of India the religions are Hinduism and Islam, but in much of this part of India the religion was Animism. This is, of course, the worship of spirits. Everything they did was related to the worship of these spirits or demons. In the plains of this part of the country they were mostly Hindus and Muslims, and in the hills and mountains they were animistic.

These mountain people were known as Nagas. They were a fierce people known for their headhunting wars between tribes. Each tribe had a portion of the mountains as their nation and this area separated India from Burma, Myanmar now.

When the British took over India they tried to control this area and said these tribes were ungovernable because they were fierce and wild. Interestingly enough, the British government made it illegal to be headhunters in 1885. The practice continued until the Gospel of the Lord Jesus was brought into this area by the early missionaries like Dr. Clark, Rev. Godhula, Dr. Bailey and others.

There are many accounts of the first contacts with the missionaries,

including one when Dr. Clark went to a village and started to speak. The chief stopped him and said that he believed like the chief in the next village. Dr. Clark said that could not be, but the chief insisted so Dr. Clark went to that village and started to give his message. About half way through he was interrupted by the chief. He asked Dr. Clark if he had seen any spirit stones in his village or any sign of spirit worship. Dr. Clark replied that he had seen nothing.

Then the chief started to tell Dr. Clark that they knew that they were all dark inside and they could do nothing to make the darkness go away. He said that he had seen a vision that there was a God that controlled everything, and that He had made some provision for the darkness in us to be made light. He then said that in the vision he had seen a white man coming with a book, and he would give them the answer to the provision of God. Then he said, "We have been waiting for all these years, and today we find out that it is Jesus God who made this provision of changing our darkness into light given by God."

That day the chief said he would follow the Jesus God that he had learned of that day. He stepped toward Dr. Clark and told him, "Today I will be a follower of this Jesus God." Almost immediately the response from the entire village was exactly the same as that of their chief. This became the first of a mass movement among the Nagas to become Christians.

This was at the end of some 10 years of ministry that was totally unfruitful, but in that tenth year there were more than 10,000 Nagas who became Christians. What a reward for so many years when there were no results. Today there are hundreds of thousands of Christians in this part of India, and it has become one of the great miracle stories in modern missions.

My mother and father answered the call to this part of India, and my father eventually founded what is today called the Northeastern Theological Seminary. Thousands of young men and women have been trained as leaders in this part of India. I am so honored to have been a boy growing up in this area which was so very wild and out of control, but I saw the power of Almighty God transform an entire area of a country.

In 1997 our son and I returned to minister to this area of India. We had the privilege of ministering to the leadership of more than 7,000 churches in that area. I told my son that when I was a boy there were human heads hanging on the walls of houses, and now these villages are Christian.

During our visit one afternoon there was an enactment of a headhunting war dance for my benefit. It was amazing to see the performance that told the story of headhunters going to war against another village. After they had finished that part of the dance the chief warrior came and challenged me to fight! He knew that I had been taught the Naga fighting dance as a boy and he wanted to see if I still remembered it. He gave me a shield and a spear and we put on a mock fight, to the joy of all that were there. It was amazing how the moves came back to me those many, many years later. By the way, he let me win, but I ended by placing my arms around him and telling him how very special he and all the Nagas were to me and to my whole family.

At the conclusion of this reenactment, the chant went out from these warriors who were now Christians, that they had been headhunters in the past, but now have become heart hunters for the Lord Jesus Christ.

What a graphic picture that told of what the Lord Jesus had done for them, changing them from being the fierce, wild Nagas into today being some of the greatest missionaries to all parts of India and the world.

So this is the end of a story of the lives of two of God's special servants, John William and Jennie Frances Cook, my dad and mom, who served the Lord along with their colleagues and saw the incredible rewards from their lives of faithfulness to the Lord Jesus Christ.

My prayer is that these stories will have caused you to go on some adventures with me as I have relived them for you. More than that is my desire that you might have been challenged to be a Christian that will live for the Lord Jesus in your life and become the champion that He has chosen you to be in the days ahead of you.

May the blessing of the Lord Jesus be your portion until the day we see Him face to face. I trust we will hear Him say to us, "W*ell done and welcome home.*"

Continue the Adventure

<u>Under His Majesty's Command, My Life's Voyage in Ministry</u>
James R. Cook

This is an auto biography by the author, especially interesting because of his relationship to Captain James Cook, the historic British explorer.

<u>Uncle Jim's Jungle Stories</u> Audio Book
James R. Cook

This is a 4-CD presentation read by the author. It is quite unique as the author uses the sounds of the jungle animals as he reads. This would be a great asset as you listen in your home or take along on a trip. It will be a challenge to your children or grandchildren as they become involved with adventure and learn Biblical principles.

<u>Village Path to the Hilltop</u>
John William Cook

This is the story of the author's father and mother, pioneer missionaries in India from the early 1930's. The book will inspire you in your life when you realize that farm young people from Minnesota and Iowa were called by the Lord into missionary service and used by Him in a tremendous way in North East India. The British government placed them in the <u>British Who's Who</u> for the next 30 years of their lives.

Contact Information:

To order one of the above go to:

tigerpawbooks@gmail.com